body jewellery

international perspectives

donald j.willcox

PITMAN PUBLISHING
39 Parker Street, London WC2B 5PB

this
book

with
love

is
for Anne —
a tiny flower with roots

and
for Walter —
a silly old tree in bloom

First published in Great Britain 1974
SIR ISAAC PITMAN AND SONS LTD.
Pitman House, Parker Street, Kingsway, London, WC2B 5PB
P.O. Box 46038, Portal Street, Nairobi, Kenya
SIR ISAAC PITMAN (AUST.) PTY. LTD.
Pitman House, 158 Bouverie Street, Carlton, Victoria 3053, Australia

Contributors

Foreword

. . . open a window,
what do you see? . . .

To open a window is to change the air. Sometimes the air inside (particularly in the mind) needs changing. There is excitement in fresh air. Can you smell it? It carries the scent of freedom, risk, discovery, and change.

I believe the pages of this book represent the opening of many mental "windows." The subject of the book is body adornment, but the pulse of the book has opened windows whenever they were closed.

Hiding behind each mental window lies a pair of eyes. Eyes are to *see* with. They are visual recording instruments for the mind. Many people, however, use their eyes only to *look*. This book represents over fifty pairs of eyes — eyes that have been trying to see.

Yes, open a window. What do you see?

Donald J. Willcox
Faaborg, Denmark

Introduction

The time it takes to plant a seed is not the time it takes to build a wall. This book is offered as a seed rather than a wall.

But even seeds take time to plant, to care for, and to mature. This book, for example, was over two years in the making. Our energy was to build a book wherein jewelry craftsmen from all parts of the world could actively exchange and share their forms, their ideas, and even their human sides — their struggles, frustrations, and defeats.

As individuals working within the same medium, we felt the need to build an alternative to what has now become almost stereotyped in jewelry crafts publishing — the step-by-step autobiographical picture book written from the viewpoint of a single author or form.

In order to make a clean break from this stereotype, we felt it was important to voice many points of view, and to do so within a loose framework — a framework where participants felt free to shout or cry, to be academic, stuffy, romantic, boring, nostalgic, gutsy, satirical, or however they honestly happened to be as individual people and as craftsmen searching for a means of expression in this, our conflicting and contradictory world. Our mutual aim, then, was to build a crafts teaching book wherein our humanness and our heartbeat were neither excluded nor omitted.

Humanness is, after all, another side of the coin to educational crafts technology. There seems to be little doubt that most of us live in a time when technology threatens to reign supreme. But to perform *technically well* is not at all the same as to perform *creatively*.

For the performing craftsman, creativity and humanness are inseparable. A technically well-executed form is still a very long way away from a form that produces a human response. Most of us have tucked something of ourselves — something very intimate — into our forms. For as long as we can make it last, we are still *people* — not machines. And since people are still the ultimate conceivers and consumers of jewelry, humanness cannot be ignored within a crafts education.

Technology is our tool, but humanness is our soul. Humanness is our attempt to put guts into our forms and to raise them up from the mire of sterile technology.

In these, the 1970s, we as a group do pretty well when it comes to learning our technical homework, but we sometimes neglect our soul. And this soul of ours needs a great deal of exercise. It gives us the ability to feel. Some of us are afraid to feel — or maybe we feel too much but just don't know how to let these feelings out.

In spite of the twentieth century, to feel is not a human deformity. The ability to feel, and to translate our feelings into meaningful forms, is what "creativity" is all about. If our technology is to be kept alive and responsible, then it needs to be fed. As craftsmen, the only food we have to feed it is the raw material of our feelings. This is the nontechnical lesson that is often overlooked within a crafts education. We believe the lesson is just as valuable to a learning experience as receiving technical instruction. And, hopefully, as we try to express ourselves in both form and words this attempt will provide an insight into what makes us tick. If nothing else, it will at least provide an opportunity to react — to more than visual form alone.

Learning experiences involve more than simply following the step-by-step instructions of one who sets himself up as an authority figure. The authority approach is the common approach, particularly within crafts publishing. But the approach is riddled with drawbacks. It not only limits alternatives, but it actually aborts much of the learning process. Each of us needs room to move. Each of us is equipped with his own measure of curiosity. This curiosity needs to be given an open window through which to see. It even needs a chance to fail. Yes, we have a right to fail. To fail by our own hand is often the most valuable learning experience we can have.

There is no single "right" way of doing any one thing. To deny this would be to deny change itself. Somebody is always coming along with an improvement or another way of doing things. Only in a book like this — in which many jewelry craftsmen expose both their forms and their voices — is there a realistic possibility of gaining an overview of any single crafts medium. If we should contradict one another in the pages that follow and conclude no single rule for thinking or for creating jewelry form, then we will have succeeded in demonstrating a slice of reality. And, hopefully, the reader will have gained something firsthand — namely, that each learning experience is as individual as each human fingerprint.

This book, then, is what we hope will be acceptable as a "craftsman's book," rather than as an "author book." To build the book, each of the participating craftsmen was invited to contribute photographs of his forms, along with explanatory captions. About 90 percent of the invited craftsmen responded. Each was encouraged to jury himself, without author-publisher judgment, or, in other words, to represent himself however he wished. He was also invited to contribute an informal essay or statement, wherein he was free to comment upon his forms, his medium, his method of working, his triumphs, his failures, or whatever else rested heavy upon his mind. The invitation for essays was prefaced only with the promise that submissions would remain unedited and with a statement that there were no rules regarding subject matter. Therefore, what you will see and read in the pages that follow is exactly the manner in which these craftsmen elected to represent themselves.

The responses arrived with every conceivable variation. Some had nothing to say, not even providing captions for their forms. Others were meticulous, fluent, soul-searching, and even self-critical. Is there a thread that ties us all together? Is there something we're trying to say or define?

The answer is yes. I think many of us feel trapped within the contradiction — or perhaps the paradox — of our medium. That we live in a troubled and very disturbed world has reached us all. Our responses are pain, sorrow, and disgust over the events of the 1970s and over the human and environmental conditions that surround us. We are reacting at all levels. We want to *say* and *do* something. Our isolation has ended. We want to make positive contributions toward reestablishing our blood ties with the world at large and toward balancing our world's precarious social and economic imbalances.

We are asking questions. We are asking where we are, and who we are. And some of us don't like our answers. We find ourselves creating expensive frills at a time when our world shows signs of falling apart. When the bellies of children remain empty, can an "exclusive" necklace help to fill them? When men are engaged in destroying each other and their environment, can a hand-made finger ring become a voice? Can body adornment really contribute to problem solving? Is jewelry perhaps unnecessary? Is it in fact a contradiction? And are we not also contradicting the things we feel? Yes, if there is a thread that ties us all together, then that thread exposes itself in the questions we ask.

And who are we as contributors? About one-third of us are teachers. We direct jewelry programs in American and European universities and in craft schools. And, as our forms bear witness, we are not *just* rhetorical people. Even though we may teach to survive, we try hard to practice what we preach. Many of us are also private craftsmen working in our own studios or operating our own shops. A few of us are students, and others among us are either engaged in museum restoration work or working in partnership with jewelry industry. Who are we? We are a blend of many talents, many voices, and many points of view within our medium. We hope we are a representation of the 1970s — an indication of where jewelry design is headed and of where we are headed.

As a name on the book cover, my own part in this venture has been to seek a new role for the crafts author. After having contributed a dozen titles to the swelling shelves of crafts books, it seemed to me that the traditional role of the crafts author was becoming an anachronism. By virtue of his "calling," a crafts author is cast in the role of a mouthpiece — a kind of third person journalist who enters the crafts picture in order to bring the message of the craftsman before the eyes of the reader. He is the translator, the interpreter, and the middleman. Sometimes we crafts authors do manage to get the message straight, but at other times we garble it completely. Our batting average is actually only mediocre. To act as middlemen has been our role for over twenty-five years. But the role is only one of many alternatives in presenting the crafts to the reader. Hopefully, this book represents a second alternative — that of allowing the craftsman to speak for himself without the middleman. My new role has therefore been a delightful learning experience, a kind of cross between a crafts author, a custodial engineer, and a private secretary. And quite frankly, I have enjoyed riding in the rumble seat in order to allow craftsmen to drive for themselves.

New Directions

"Newness" is an overworked, ambiguous term. What is new to one individual may be tired or traditional to another. The work of a California craftsman who creates body form from feathers is called "new," but the black Nigerian craftsman sees nothing new in using feathers. For him, decorative body feathers are as traditional as the rhythms of his ancestry. With only a few exceptions, one could draw similar analogies for most other jewelry materials. The same is true for form and for the placement of jewelry form on the body. One can find close similarities that dispel nearly all claims of "newness" — whether the similarities come from forms in the natural world or from manmade objects, as for example, in the similarities between an Etruscan body form dating from 600 years before Christ and a wrap-around body form from the 1970s. The individual definition of newness is therefore in direct proportion to the width of perspective the craftsman has upon his medium.

Our crafts language is saturated with ambiguous terms. For example, one hears, and finds himself using, such terms as "experimental," "modern," and "contemporary." The attempt, in using these terms, is to define the new directions reflected by craftsmen of the 1970s. What we are trying to do through linguistics is to differentiate our new forms from our old forms — to find a way to lump everything new into a single category so as not to confuse or include it with the categories of the past. Terms such as "body adornment" or "body jewelry" are directed toward this same end, even though everyone realizes that the body has been a major consideration of jewelry design for thousands of years. The point is that our language is just too limited and too worn to catch exactly the nuances of definition that we are trying to capture. What we want as younger form-makers is a way to describe the change in our current mentality — away from the doodad, gimcrack, and sugar-frosted forms of the past thirty years. We want a way to say: "Look here, world — our heads have changed. There's more to be said than the weight and price of the material." We're trying hard to find our human and artistic conscience, but unfortunately our language just hasn't given us a ready-made word or phrase with which to say this. So the tiptoe, tightrope-walking word game continues.

Perhaps, from a historical perspective, it is accurate to say that the craftsmen of the 1970s are beginning a period of rediscovery: a rediscovery of human values, artistic values, technical values, form values, and raw material values. Our rediscoveries are in harmony with similar value rediscoveries going on all around us. For many of us, it's as if we've just come through (and thankfully survived) a kind of sleeping sickness, an artistic lethargy, or an extraordinarily overdelayed birth-giving within our medium.

Gone is our sleeping sickness, and high are the spirits. Gone is the lethargy, and clear is the head. The shades have been lifted and the rulebooks have been burned. Oh yes, we still have our daily individual ups and downs, but the spirit of the medium is different now. We are excited, smiling, energy-filled, with ideas popping, places to go, and roads to travel upon. We are enjoying our medium like a kid enjoys an ice cream cone on a hot summer day. A little of all of this is in our work, and our forms celebrate the event. This is the basis for our rediscovery — our new direction.

What many of us are doing is moving away from the old mentality of baubles and bangles — or better yet, away from the precious and semiprecious globs of material that we used to fasten or stick onto people like warts or like cancerous growths that the human body would instinctively reject. We went through a long, tiresome period where "jewelry" was defined in terms of its material value. The bigger the glop of gold, the better the piece. The thicker the jewel frosting, the higher we rose in the eyes of our covetous neighbors. It was like heaping perfectly beautiful raw material up in mounds that often looked like the mounds outside a farmer's barn. A lot of people still haven't moved away from this value judgment, but they will. It takes time to change.

During this period, most of what was handmade or intentionally conceived belonged exclusively to the rich, unless one had a great-grandmother or a secret admirerer. What the man on the street bought for his wife or sweetheart was about on the same level as what one now buys in Woolworth's at the costume jewelry counter. More garbage! But at least the Woolworth variety was cheap, and maybe it was more honest than dung-piles of gold.

But then something happened. Maybe we form-makers had just reached a dead end, or maybe we had grown sick of ourselves and sick of our role. At any rate, we began to poke our noses out from our caves of mental hibernation, and we started to do something positive.

At first we still treated a form as something to dangle or stick onto somebody. Although we slowly began to change our techniques and materials, our forms were still independent objects to hang on the body like a cow bell. We were still hassled by the inescapable chain, which seemed to be our only solution for linking the human form to the jewel form. But at least we were trying. We were beginning to rediscover that anything was a potential material for body adornment.

At first public reaction was filled with its usual extremes of liberalism and conservatism. On the one hand, the public scratched its head, raised its eyebrows, and panned that "knowing" look that says, "Better to call the men in the white coats." But on the other extreme, particularly among gallery people, the air of change was welcome and in some cases brought dollar signs to the eyeballs. It was the generation gap all over again. Young eyes were eager for change, but older eyes needed a bit more time to digest what was going on.

As soon as the noses (from those of us who had poked them into rediscovery) began to feel a positive response, the whole door of rediscovery was flung wide open — literally ripped off its hinges. This is the nature of encouragement in all human endeavor. When the first few craftsmen discovered that their loneliness was shared by others, and that they weren't as kooky, or as nuts, as they sometimes even suspected themselves, the nose-poking changed into a foot-stomping. Jewelry design was coming alive.

A lot of crazy and not so crazy things were happening in the related arts during this same time, and many of these happenings spilled over into jewelry. There was a time in the 1950s and 1960s when jewelry experienced many of the same offshoots as did art and sculpture. Many craftsmen found themselves involved in a kind of optical, pop, protest, and even junk or collage form-building. If this offshoot didn't last long, it at least encouraged the rediscovery of dormant materials and of the techniques necessary to handle these materials.

All types of nontraditional materials and combinations of material were rediscovered for form building. Once the rulebooks were burned, only the sky was the limit. Wood, glass, ceramics, leather, fur, acryl, feathers, cork, bone, horn, iron, stainless steel, aluminum, paper, tin, pewter, brass, copper, fabric, enamel, common stone, fossil, and dozens of fibers — from hemp, silk, wool, and nylon to sisal — began to find acceptance in building body form. Silver, gold, and other precious and semiprecious material began a transformation away from their traditional use. Silver and transparent acryl in the same form? Unheard of! But it worked. Gold and wood? Amber and iron? Diamonds and granite? Amethyst and leather? Pearls and hemp? It all happened and, again, most of it worked. The direction was to rediscover unused form materials, explore inexpensive materials, and reevaluate the tired truisms that had for so long dictated rules about how materials should be used. Obviously, these changes screwed a lot of heads on in another way — craftsmen began to see, conceive, evaluate, and think differently. But it has all come to pass, and most of it proudly.

Forms began to grow larger, bolder — even "dangerous." Forms began to grow onto and into the human body as if they belonged there. The body was being rediscovered, and jewelry was being redefined. Yes, we had always considered the body, but we had too often defined it in terms of confining our forms. We didn't dare make a ring too large. A lady might not be able to fit her gloves on over it. We didn't dare build a bold form on the breast. A lady might not be able to fit her fur coat on over it. What had we done? We had mistakenly defined the body in a way that made it necessary to limit our jewelry.

But as soon as our rediscovery began, we learned our mistake. *We*, not the body, had made the rules. *We* had done the confining; the body was free. And it wasn't only the neck, the wrist, the ears, and the fingers that could support jewelry form. No, the chest, the back, the breasts, the face, and even the legs and head became fair game for form. If a pendant could lie on the chest, then why couldn't two pendants be joined at the shoulders so that one could lie on the back? And why couldn't forms be interchanged? Who said that an armband always had to be worn at the wrist? Could it not equally be worn at the upper arm or on the leg? And why couldn't we leave room in our forms for the consumer's fantasy? Why couldn't we give him a choice to wear our forms however he wished?

As rediscovery progressed there were, of course, the inevitable technical problems that popped up as growing pains. These had to be confronted and solved. Many of the first growing forms turned out to be completely impractical to wear. They were too heavy. They had sharp edges or angles that caught on clothing. And they were often too difficult to get in and out of. But the growing pains were highly individual. Serious craftsmen dug in and solved the functional problems just as quickly as they came up. Heavy materials were often replaced by lighter ones. In some situations weight was reduced by laminating or hollowing out the forms. Forms also became smoother, even convex, to form against the body. And fastening systems became less complicated and more functional.

This rediscovery of materials brought the craftsman way outside the traditional realm of the gold and silversmith. The artist was now dealing with nonprecious materials, and he had to learn how to use them. He had to spill himself over into many nonjewelry craft areas in order to learn techniques. An unbelievable amount of human energy had to be invested in learning and in rediscovering that nothing could be taken for granted. But the learning process was like a prairie fire fanned by wind. Each new technical problem brought the craftsman closer to his material. An intimate exchange was going on. The more he enriched himself with technical knowledge, the closer he grew to understanding the nature of each material.

The jewelry craftsman, this artistic phenomenon of the 1970s who had inherited a mountain of tradition, began to crochet, knit, embroider, braid, knot, weave, cast, oxidize, color, engrave, photoelectroplate, carve, weld, solder, polish, lacquer, twist, hammer, bend, cement, laminate, spin, and enamel materials that were completely new to him in a jewelry context. No stone was left unturned in order to create change within the medium.

And then the male came into the picture. Our dull, half-neglected male, who had dressed himself like a penguin for nearly half a century, came into view for body form. And he didn't seem to mind at all — in fact, after he got used to it, he too seemed to wonder why he had misplaced his tail feathers for so long. The male (bless his heart) produced new markets for the jewelry craftsman. In the penguin days, the male consumption of jewelry had been limited to the backbone of safety: tie-clips, cufflinks, and rings (provided these were small in size, but still glittery enough to look valuable). Many men — often even businessmen — turned in their striped neckties and replaced them with breast pendants. And then belt buckles, clasps, and leather accessories (especially shoulder bags and belt bags) became a new market for the jewelry form-maker to invest energy in. And he did. Dozens of craftsmen are still heavily into exploring these forms for men. We hope the activity continues.

On the feminine side, the mood for consuming the craftsman's fantasy has also been entirely positive. At the beginning of the 1970s there were thousands of women who welcomed eagerly the chance to wear bolder-form, nonprecious material and forms designed for unusual placement on the body. By the beginning of the 1970s, materials such as fiber, leather, fur, ceramic, acryl, glass, wood, aluminum, stainless steel, and iron were acceptable as fashion. The same was true for jewelry for the upper arm, the leg, the head, and the breasts. There are even garment vest forms.

Like the craftsman, the public has also changed. A skeptical, slow-changing craftsman can no longer rely upon total public conservatism. In many situations, particularly in fashion, the consumer is even more willing to accept change than is the craftsman. When a public can accept the reality of a man on the moon, rhetoric about the aesthetics of an acryl armband as opposed to a gold armband becomes absurd. The conservative of today is in no way the conservative of yesterday.

The existing partnership between the jewelry designer and jewelry industry has also helped to change the public head. Designer-craftsmen working with industry have managed to market excellent form in series, thereby providing bolder form for a mass audience at lower prices.

Scandinavia stands as a rich example of this partnership, and the Finnish firm Kruunu Koru is the unequaled leader in the field. In the early part of the 1960s, Finnish goldsmith Bjorn Weckstrom was alone when he began breaking the rules of tradition. After a number of setbacks, Bjorn finally attracted some mild attention when his forms won a couple of international jewelry prizes. This break elevated his work from the "unsafe" to at least the "questionable." A short time later, Bjorn managed to form a working partnership with the small Helsinki firm Kruunu Koru. The atmosphere of the partnership was entirely positive. This small firm believed in Weckstrom, believed in change, and supported Weckstrom by answering "yes" to the ideas he came up with for form and material. The word "impossible" was not part of the Kruunu Koru vocabulary. The firm proceeded under the assumption that all problems contained solutions. This positive partnership grew, swelled, and then became a giant. By 1970 Kruunu Koru was one of the largest series producers of silver and gold in the world. Today the firm employs over seventy gold and silversmiths, and has opened its doors to several other talented form-makers. And the beautiful part of the whole experience is that the growth came as a direct result of breaking tradition. The firm began producing Weckstrom's bold "Space-Silver" forms at a time when most other firms were still producing bowling badges and necktie clips. And by the time the competition began to open its eyes to change and to follow the Weckstrom lead, Kruunu Koru was producing Weckstrom's silver and acryl forms and experimenting with electroplated copper for series production. There is no question that this type of series production in non-traditional form and material has helped to nail down the message of change right at the pocketbook level, where change is understood by the greatest number in the shortest possible time.

If conservatism still exists within the production-selling-buying cycle, then the public is by no means the only contributor. In most cases, the disciples of safety are the very same salesmen and retailers who are supposedly one of the key outlets for new form. At a time when mass communication is available at the flick of an electric switch and when the dictates of fashion saturate our daily existence, the conservative retailer and his salesmen too often still prefer hiding behind the safety of charm bracelets and cameo rings. These people should be thoroughly spanked, particularly by craftsmen.

And where are we moving now? Hopefully, the pages of this book will provide a few road signs. We are crocheting fine silver wire into breast forms, constructing earrings out of glass eyeballs, electrifying our pendants with transistor cells, knotting rope into vest forms, gluing feathers and fur onto belts, setting amber in iron, carving acryl into rings, attaching badges and coins to wood, fabricating photographic images onto silver — yes, we are moving in all directions.

Our forms are growing and approaching garment proportions. Many of us are trying to bridge the gap between a piece of jewelry and a garment. Our forms are becoming garmentlike. Not only are we seeking to master our own medium, but we are poking our noses out again, into the sanctuary of the fashion designer. We have served our apprenticeship, mastered it well, and matured in our medium. We no longer feel confined by limited definitions in how we express ourselves.

What is jewelry? Where does jewelry end and clothing begin? Perhaps these are questions that will ultimately have no meaning — no answer. And who will mourn the passing of gift-wrapped answers, tidy boxes of "truth," and rhetorical clichés? Were not they, like the Great White Whale and the Abominable Snowman, figments of fantasy?

Yes, we have peacocked ourselves with frosted glitter for centuries. Monarchs and madmen alike, we have hoarded, and gorged ourselves with, precious material. Our judgments have been based upon rarity and upon economics. We have accepted and applauded crap — provided it cost enough and aroused the envy of our neighbors. And we have paid a dear price. Our craftsmen have been pawns on a chessboard, to be moved about at the whim of wealth. But we have finally thrown up the crap, and we doubt that we will be easily harnessed again.

Perhaps the monarchs and madmen of the future will be hoarding and gorging themselves with feathers, iron, acryl, and fiber. And perhaps their reasons for hoarding will be related to form, craftsmanship, and the expression of ideas rather than with material value. We may well fail to abolish man's greed, but we can at least hope to improve upon the quality of his judgment.

body
jewellery

John Houston
England

To fill a book on jewelry with only a jewelry craftsman's point of view is stacking the deck. When many craftsmen all jump in to let off steam and to let the chips fall where they may, we of course risk losing part of our overview. God forbid that this effort mutate into a "crying towel" therapy session for myopic jewelry craftsmen!

In order to keep a sense of intelligent perspective, I have therefore invited John Houston, the curator of London's Goldsmith's Hall, to be our first contributor. Most of us may *think* we know where we're at, but how often do we really see ourselves as others see us? John Houston sees us. He sees us every day of his working life, and he represents one of the "organization men" whose task it is to deal with us and try to make sense out of what we're doing and where we're headed.

More often than not, we don't give the John Houstons a fair shake. We tend to slump them off, ignore them, and often even credit them only as if they were the very personification of the devil himself: the institution man, the authority man, the critic, the man who doles out the prizes, the man with the key to our bank, the decision man, and sometimes, the man most responsible for boiling our bloodstreams.

But how often is our sizing up of the John Houstons only a private perspective? How often do we see the whole parade of the jewelry medium marching before our eyes? People like John Houston do see the *whole* parade. Maybe many of the Johns are blind in one eye and unable to see from the other, but Curator Houston is not among them. John Houston is a sniffer, a digger, and his senses are vibrating. Here's what John has to say.

Institutional patronage smacks of committees, mediocrity, and pomposity. The only antidote to these killer diseases is a reckless trust in the best. Almost inevitably, the most creative artist in any medium tends to be feckless about money, absurdly optimistic about delivery dates, and ruthlessly experimental, seldom repeating successes and therefore constantly shattering his patron's preconceptions. These remarks emerge from bitter individual experience — each adjective is linked to disastrous anecdote, much too libelous to print.

The Worshipful Company of Goldsmiths is an eight-centuries-old City of London Livery Company, born as a medieval craft guild — part trade union, part trade association. Linked to a craft that still operates on a human scale after four centuries, the company is a unique survival, busy today administering charitable funds, assisting schools, colleges, and universities, and helping to cajole, convince, and commission the best possible work from modern goldsmiths, silversmiths, and jewelers.

The process of public patronage — gift-giving in fancy dress — confers a mysterious ceremonial order on the creative process of the designer. First, there is the motive: one institution wishes to honor another, to please or persuade or merely to mark the inexorable passage of time that dignifies power and invents tradition.

Enter the designer, in his dual role of victim and therapist, to face a committee nervous at a new venture, a committee probably composed of bankers, accountants, professors, or politicians, each familiar with facts, ready to digest, report, lecture, but unused to decisions being embodied in an aesthetic object. So inevitably they talk about money, professional obligations, delivery dates, rejection fees, and purchase tax. The designer must act within this network, be persuasive, convincing, all things to some men — and yet remain true to himself.

Then everyone waits. The designer digests his ideas. His patrons fear the worst: he may be struck by lightning, get married, become bankrupt, or lose interest. Amazingly he appears with his proposed designs. These may be original, that is, unfamiliar to his patrons. They ask for some simple fruit bowls, heavy silver, discreetly decorative, unexceptionable; but the designer offers three undulating concavities, hyperbolic paraboloids stressed and striped in silver and gilt to the tension of a catenary curve. Explanations follow: the designer had visited the intended recipient, a northern university, studied the landscape, drawn the buildings, related the two, and infused geology with mathematics to a unique flavor. His conviction was successfully infectious.

In Britain the craft of British metals spawns blank kinds of artists. The artist-craftsman, blending his manual skills with autograph idiosyncrasies, draws his strength from a century-old tradition of technical simplicity, often strained through the fine mesh of Bauhaus analysis. At its worst, this produces hard edges in soft metal; at best, it results in forms pressured by individual experiment yet tempered with domestic delight. A second type is the poor designer, too often unsullied by any contact with reality. His ideas remain pen and paper arbitrary forms, brutally imposed on misunderstood traditions. Finally, there is the maverick, often self-made or moving horizontally across a wider plateau of skills. Often beginning as painter, architect, gunsmith, or engineer. Frequently, bringing not only a freshness of approach but also a completely new range of ideas and attitudes, sometimes rooted in metalwork traditions — Egyptian, Oriental, or medieval — ignored by the present-day industry. The successful survivors of this dangerous transfer (and a bad painter makes a bad jeweler) create uncopyable idioms: they are the ones that turn craft into art.

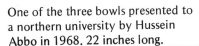

One of the three bowls presented to a northern university by Hussein Abbo in 1968. 22 inches long.

Steeplechase trophy. Etched and oxidized silver. *Hussein Abbo*, 1968. 18 inches long.

Cigar jar in deeply carved steel with partially silvered and gilded surfaces. *Malcolm Appleby*, 1969. 12 inches tall. Appleby infiltrated many art schools, emerged without a single qualification, and has worked as a gunsmith engraver, a die-cutter, and a jeweler. He is currently absorbed in a vast steel and silver chess set which, according to John Houston, "does for that game what Tolkien did for Iniguisties." Appleby lives in a rail-less railroad station in the Scottish highlands and appears irregularly in London with his knapsack and pockets swollen and sagging with his work.

Prototype copper jugs for a university commission. *Paul Harrison.* These first ideas were quirkily bird-like. The shovellike spouts are not only nondrip, but also graded so that liquid will pour gently.

18-carat green gold necklace with silver-pink freshwater pearls. *Louis Osman.* Whereas some fine designers and superb craftsmen preserve a pure stream of originality, Osman is a torrent, tearing at the past, uprooting the future in a maelstrom of mud and stones, mixing metaphors, inventing analogies — infinitely inventive.

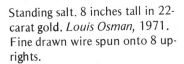

Standing salt. 8 inches tall in 22-carat gold. *Louis Osman,* 1971. Fine drawn wire spun onto 8 uprights.

After lengthy discussion and discretion, the jug prototypes ended up as four dignified silver jugs — still birdlike, but pigeons rather than predators. *Paul Harrison.*

Heikki M. Seppa

United States

While Heikki and I were corresponding before his contribution, one of his letters suddenly exploded on the subject of crafts publishing. His language is vivid. I believe his words are worth sharing.

I think we are right in trying to break the "book-to-impress-other-craftsmen" syndrome in publishing. What we need is a good soul-searching book, or an absolutely matter-of-fact, nonemotional book. Everything in the library now seems to be in the wishy-washy middle. Nobody reads it. I discourage my students from using any book. I get better results by my own methods than by having to argue the "merits" of another mind.

Total void in the area of crafts motivation is another of the sore spots. There is no book on the market which attempts to clarify the tremendous need for mind-material coexistence in our lives. The number of lunatics is increasing because the one trustworthy commodity — matter and knowledge of it — is disappearing from our lives. We have to remember that ideas still need a medium through which to be manifested. Otherwise — no ideas. All of the emotional crap that floats around in the arts nowadays rightly belongs to the aficionados and critics, not to the artists. The understanding of the damned word "art" is no more than understanding where the line between natural and manmade lies, and then substituting the latter with the word "art." If this is unacceptable, then art must be some sort of a myth, or an outright accolade that one applies to good manmade stuff.

I hope this book in hand is going to be a reality to the senses without the usual mellifluous lies and fabricated afterthoughts about the contents.

A person doesn't need decoration; an attire may need some, but not a person. Decoration be damned! Beauty be damned! The refinement of ideas — either the maker's or the onlooker's (it doesn't matter which) — should be the purpose of jewelry. The question should be, Can you invest an idea in this ring? not, Does it *look* good? People are not mannequins, they are individuals. They are the ones attaching value to a piece. Therefore, the ring should fit a person's mind first — then his finger.

The attitude of creative people toward their patrons is often pathetically subservient. "I like your stuff," the patron says. "Thank you," goes the melon-mouthed genius. "This other ring, however, stinks!" "Oooo, I'm sorry," goes the people-pleaser.

Craftsmen often prove themselves to be very bad businessmen by being too eager to please any fib of a patron's imagination. The most successful craftsmen (in business terms) have formulated premeditated procedural patterns to keep them out of trouble. These include avoiding the necessity of making policy in the heat of the negotiations. A fast-talking patron can make a craftsman run like a headless chicken.

Everybody has creativity. The only problem is that it lies buried, inhibited, and hampered by conventions, habit, and selection of the wrong medium. What art schools can do is create a situation where a person can find his own medium or media and rid himself of his fixed ideas. And after school has been left behind the going gets tough. Many compromises must be weighed; motivation changes from praise to a monetary system; ideas are not flowing around as freely; dialogue with colleagues decreases; and the atmosphere is more empty.

Gold fibula cast. The fibula, the forerunner of the modern safety pin, can take many forms as a decorative object while still functioning as a safety pin.

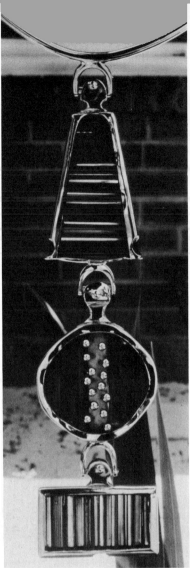

Natural tourmaline sticks used in a
gold setting. Three-part pendulum
joined by a universal joint that
allows free movement of the parts.

Cultured pearl earrings framed in
gold.

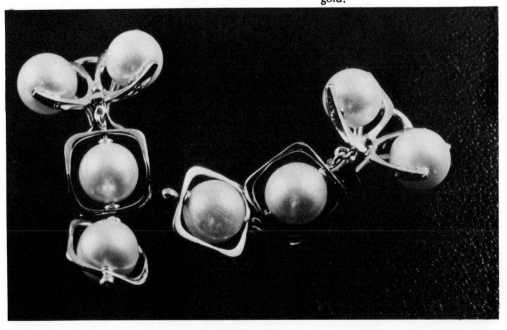

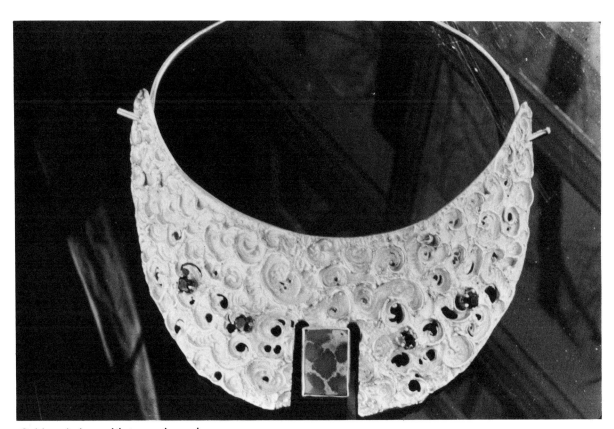

Gold neckpiece with turquoise and
garnets.

Barbara Gasch
Germany

Glass eyeballs and silver? Can such a combination of materials work as jewelry? Well, Barbara Gasch believes it can.

Sometimes I feel that making jewelry is a kind of modern antiquity. To me, it provides a fantastic outlet for meaningful work — a tiny slice of paradise in an age otherwise dominated by super industry, heavy profitmaking, and the other accompanying impersonalisms and manipulations of our capitalistic system.

Being a goldsmith allows an alternative. I can still identify myself with my work; I can still decorate myself and my friends however I want; I can still create forms of "magic" or "cultic" character; and I can still encourage and stimulate others to follow in my footsteps.

But because I must live off my work, my forms also become sales objects to be cast within the mercantile system. I often have to fight with officialdom and with snobs. And I'm often misused as a kind of purveyor to a high society whose pretensions for prestige I end up satisfying with jewelry of "imperishable value."

Belt in silver with emerald eye.

Gold ring with an enstatite. A small emerald ring appears on one of the fingers.

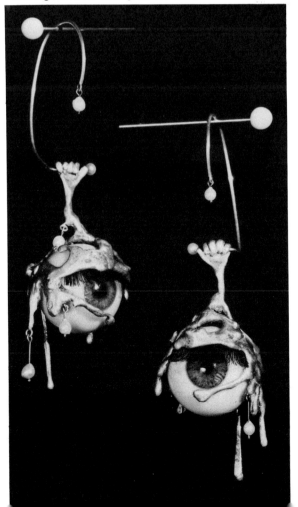

Earrings in silver with glass eyeballs.

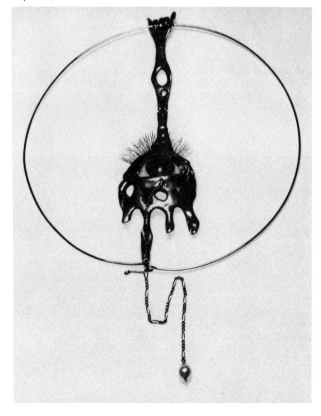

Oxidized silver pendant with glass eyeball.

11

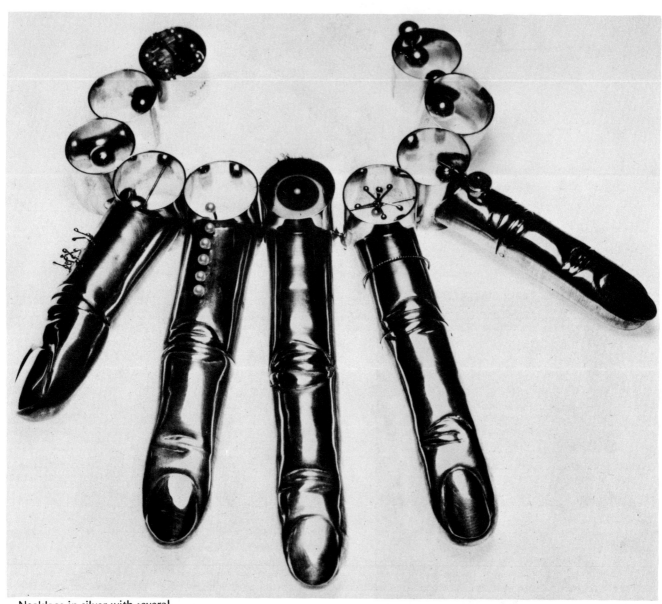

Necklace in silver with several
stones and pearls.

Fabricated silver brooch with glass eyeball.

Fabricated gold ring.

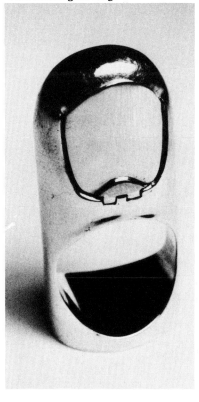

Fabricated gold ring, second view. The fingernail opens to reveal pearls.

Inge Augustin
Germany

Inge Augustin says that she tries to make her jewelry "magic, beautiful, and if possible, also a little cruel." Her husband Ernst is a novelist. In describing her work, Inge contributes an excerpt from her husband's novel *Mama,* published in 1972 by Suhrkamp Publishers of West Germany. The excerpt follows.

There have been men that could not bear an unmasked contact — strong men, military commanders — that have seen the *virgin*, but have immediately fallen down.

And it is no exaggeration to say that when the gate opens — one sees *her* standing there — well over six feet tall. Oh, her garment is like a cylinder. Her face is like . . . does she have a face? She has only a head that grows out from her shoulders. It's very painted. Her mouth is like a red rose. It reveals an invitation — a wish. The invitation is to kiss the virgin.

Oh, just the thought. That she stands down there in the cellar six feet tall and painted — it makes men fall down — men with strong hearts. Even to pronounce her name is enough to make them die.

But how is the reality?

It is an error. The golden tips of her toes reach too far out from her hemline. One can see that the toes are artificial. A real foot stands behind her.

An executioner, who stands in front to the right, and wears a squashed felt hat (that follows his ears in two equal flaps) says to the condemned: "Come forward, and greet the virgin!" But there is no response. One can see that her breast is formed inside-out. In other words, where she should have been convex, she is concave. And in the hollow parts, one could swear that there were fissures.

"Go forward — all three to the virgin," says the executioner as he thumps his lance against the floor.

Thump. Thump.

But it's impossible. Under no circumstances can the men move closer, because they know exactly what waits in store for them if they kiss the virgin.

The arms hang down from her shoulders — a fine piece of blacksmith work. Above, comes a hand-hammered hairstyle with four mother-of-pearl horns — the fantasy of a make-up artist — and it's — my God — it's Our Lady as she really is.

In spite of it all, she's still great to look at — head to toe in the finest of ornamental iron. And partly, where the iron is pierced, one can look right inside her, and see something bright — something frightening and bright.

The executioner thumps his lance again on the floor. He already knows how this thing will end.

Thump. Thump.

Now which one is the general? Which one the businessman, and which one the doctor? Which one of you will go first?

"No," says the executioner still playing his games. "All three of you will go forward at the same time, my little men. The lady is not what you think — so just get moving. Careful, there's still one more iron step — ahhh, now go and kiss the virgin."

Finally, all three of them step up and kiss the virgin. The contact causes her to buzz. Something is going on inside her. She lifts and closes her iron arms — those iron arms with iron sleeves and a fine embroidered hammer and sickle. The movement looks like a love embrace around the three men — all at once.

As she slowly squeezes her arms, long, thin spears begin growing forward, and out from the fissures in her breasts. Just as these spikes begin to pierce the proud hearts of the three men, another hunting spear slides silently out from the virgin's stomach and slices the men into halves.

Pendant of brass with enamel
settings and a rock crystal.

Pendant of gold with amethysts and
lapis lazuli. Face in ceramic; landscape settings in enamel.

Pendant of silver, ceramic, and both
baroque and "granite" pearls.

16

`Pendant of silver, ceramic, enamel, baroque pearls.

Pendant of brass and lapis lazuli with 4 enamel settings.

17

Albert R. Paley
United States

These photographs of my forms represent my investigation into the various conceptual areas of bodily adornment. In my work, I strive toward a harmony among the various elements of the piece — hopefully where the structural, decorative, and necessary mechanisms become one, or are incorporated with equal emphasis, rather than being subordinated to a hierarchy of image. Structural, three-dimensional form, not graphic facsimile, is inherent in the application of the metal working processes to the jewelry form.

Visual and structural complexity is sought with the utilization of various metal working processes within one piece. Each retains its unique character and independence while simultaneously relating to the total unit. Color is a major emphasis in my work, and I use it to accent or direct movement of form by the use of contrasting materials in metallic and nonmetallic inlay, stone, shell, or crystal formation. Patination is used specifically with gold and silver to heighten contrast and to render a permanency and durability of surface, thereby avoiding a continual maintenance just in order to preserve the original statement. This also explains my preference for nonephemeral materials in relationship to permanency. Over the years, my work has increased in scale directed toward a greater relationship with bodily forms — not in subordination as a body covering, but as objects relating directly to mass and contour. When not worn, an object should not necessarily refer to front, back, or side, but be a continuous structure.

Metal should be utilized to its full potential and not determined by quasi-technical aesthetics. These are undue restrictions upon the craftsman.

I do not work to create objects but to explore and investigate various problems. The object is merely a by-product or residue of that energy and thought process. Continual freedom is sought with the material by acquiring and perfecting skills and challenging restrictions and prerequisites, whether it be a dogmatic aesthetic or a manufactured mechanical mechanism or element. Every line, surface, color, mechanism, and structure should be challenged, and not docilely accepted — should generate its own uniqueness and validity to exist. If not, there is no use in making it.

Brooch of fabricated silver and
gold. Worn above the breast by
means of a flexible hanging element
that allows the form to conform to
the body. Materials include 5
synthetic sapphires, 3 tourmalines,
oxidized silver with striped gold
inlay, and white delrin.

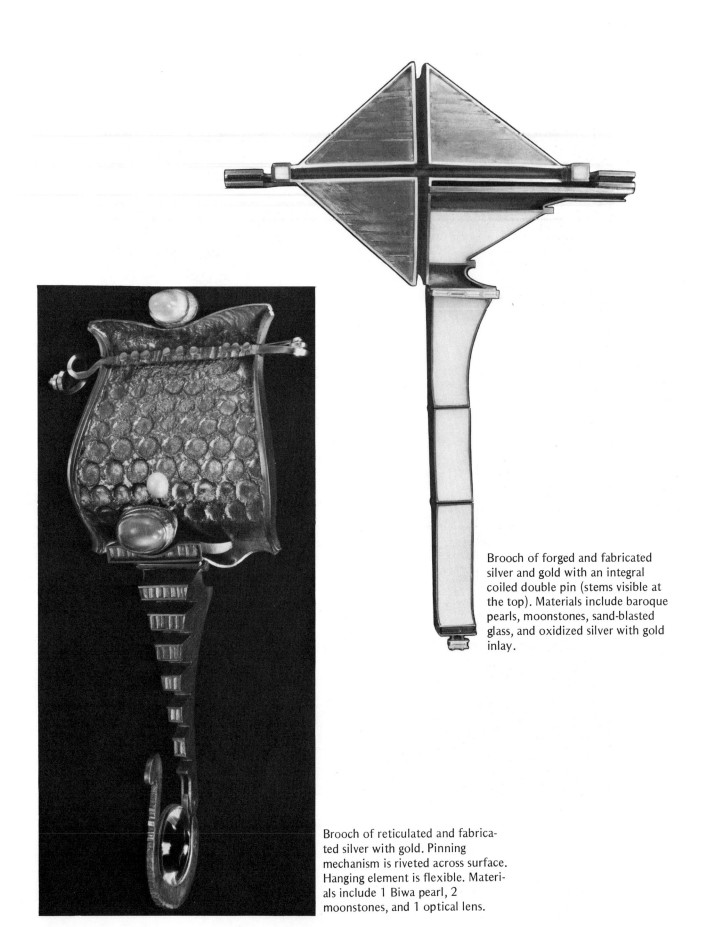

Brooch of forged and fabricated silver and gold with an integral coiled double pin (stems visible at the top). Materials include baroque pearls, moonstones, sand-blasted glass, and oxidized silver with gold inlay.

Brooch of reticulated and fabricated silver with gold. Pinning mechanism is riveted across surface. Hanging element is flexible. Materials include 1 Biwa pearl, 2 moonstones, and 1 optical lens.

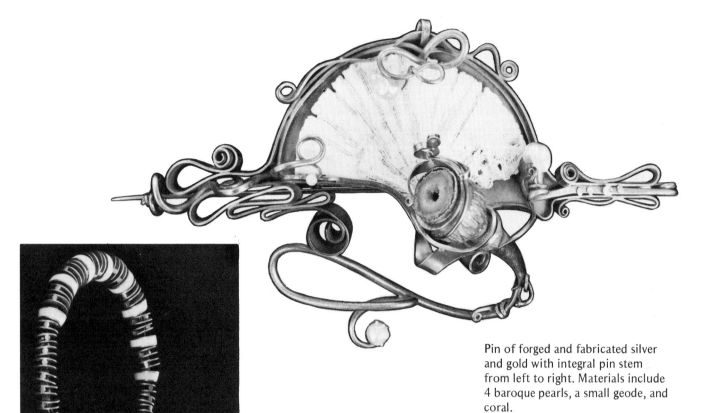

Pin of forged and fabricated silver and gold with integral pin stem from left to right. Materials include 4 baroque pearls, a small geode, and coral.

Pendant of fabricated and inlaid gold, silver, and copper with pearls, carved delrin, and antique cameo. The hollow pendant is made in 3 sections and has a flexible neck-piece.

Charlotte De Syllas
England

Dear Mr. Willcox:

I am enclosing photographs of two jobs, along with explanatory captions.

I have nothing to say in words.

Armband in forged steel with amethyst carved head. Armband also includes charcoal-colored bronze with silver lining. Cord is silk, and beads are amethyst.

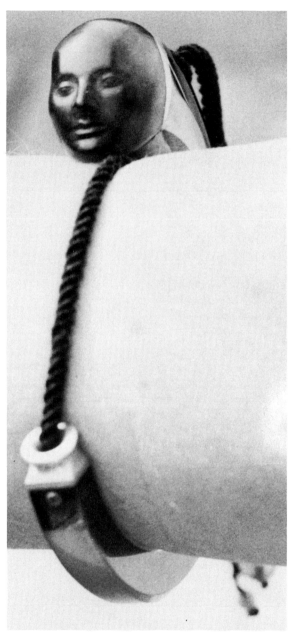

Detail, armband.

Detail, armband closing mechanism.

23

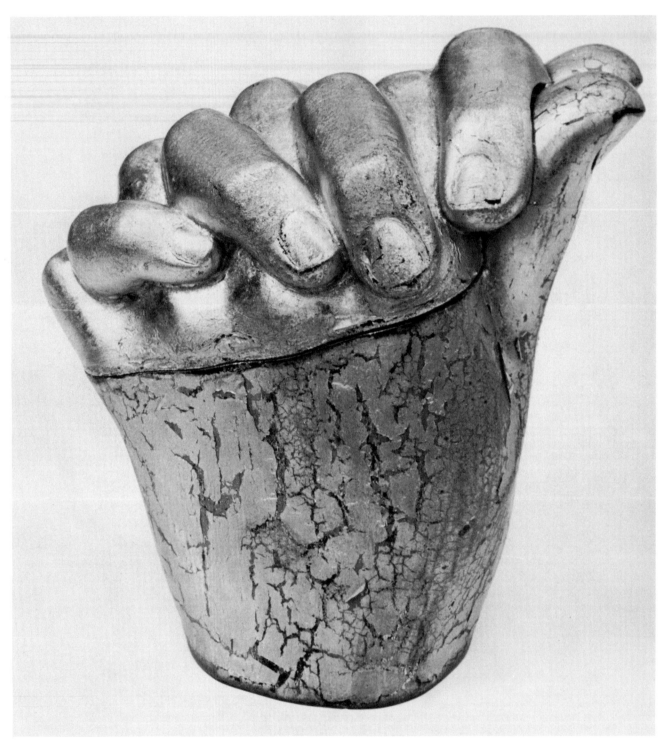

Partridge wood ring box covered in
gold leaf.

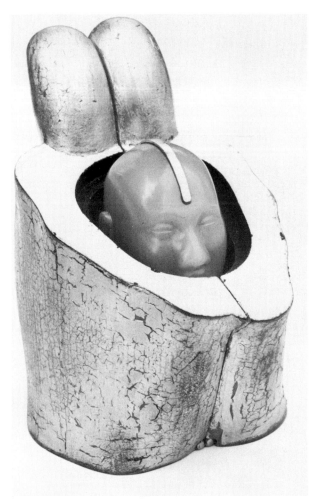

Ring box cover lifts off to reveal
ring nestled inside.

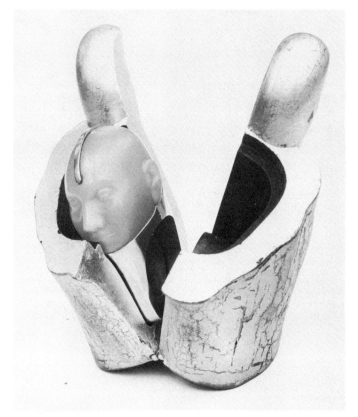

Ring box is hinged at the base.

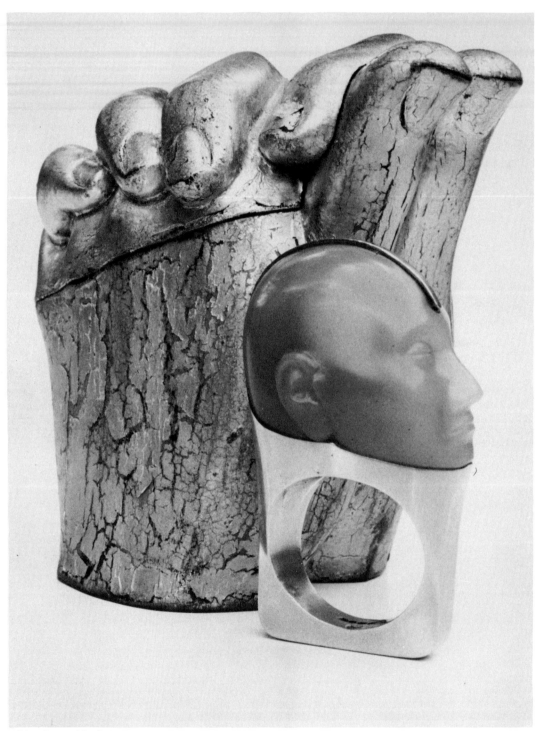

Ring box with ring.

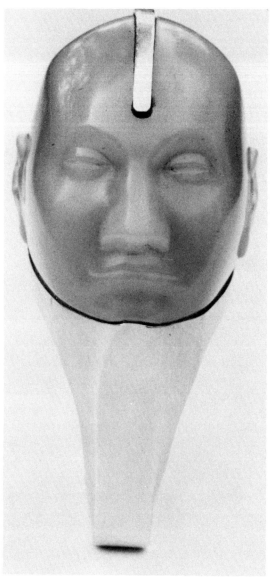

Ring, front view. The ring is carved
from chalcedony and set in yellow
gold.

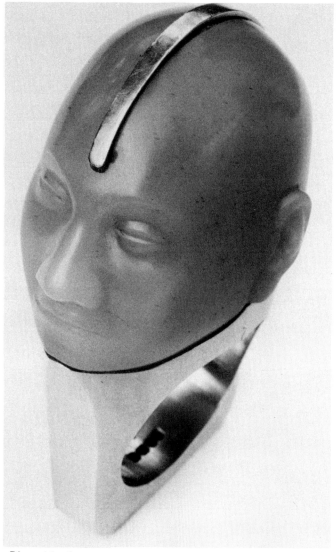

Ring, side view.

Lynda Watson

United States

I am graphically oriented. I really love to draw, and I simply can't get behind sculpture at all. Pieces which can work and be somewhat feat end up that way, usually highly decorative or somehow embellished. I love details, and I don't really care if anybody sees them as long as I know the details are there. I do "things," or somewhat predetermined shapes. I don't like globby accidental organic stuff at all. I don't make anything that I wouldn't wear myself. If I didn't have me to make jewelry for, I probably wouldn't make jewelry at all. Lots of my stuff carries itself to the point of being unwearable, but that's irrelevant as long as I'd like to wear it.

Wax lends itself very well to my design specifications, and casting — in conjunction with fabrication — make the possibilities limitless.

I'm presently teaching full time in college (a small, rural school). I really enjoy the actual teaching, but extra administrative responsibilities are a drag. Student contact fosters new ideas and provides audience and a live response for each new thing I do. As a means for getting money to do my work, it's the best job I've ever had.

"Landscape." Cast in sterling silver from extruded wax wire and sheet wax actually drawn with the wire. The pendant contains between 30 and 40 separate pieces, which were linked together after casting.

28

Before I started teaching, I had a jewelry business in Long Beach, California. I made a good living doing commissions, but I hated making things to other people's specifications. I am financially free from commissions now and do very few.

I am constantly appalled at the general public's lack of taste. I avoid street shows and fairs like the plague, and have much disdain for jewelry and other "things" made without artistic motivation. I do enjoy good shows and people who are really involved — involved at least occasionally. I have a super nice place to live and work, and look forward to blocks of time when I can devote all my energy to the sun and my work.

"Garden." Cast in silver from wax wire. There is no back up sheet. The free-swinging figures were first carved from wax.

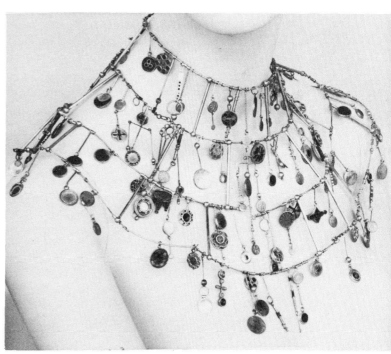

Fabricated silver and enamel neck-piece. Each separate pendant is enameled in bright colors. Lynda says that the piece "was built as an adventure in structure — it just grew and grew." Each of the parts moves independent of the others.

29

Eric Spiller
England

In the spring of 1972, Eric Spiller sat for his final examination at London's Royal College of Art, thereby completing seven years of academic "art education" and earning himself a master of arts degree. He contributes the following about himself and his work.

Most of my work conforms to the traditional concept of jewelry only insofar as it shares the functional aspect and is meant to be worn. The emphasis is on aesthetic value rather than on the material worth established by the rarity of materials employed.

I want people to consume my work on its own merit and not in comparison with formal, traditional jewelry, although it does often conform to similar functional aspects. In a tentative way, I attempt this segregation by calling an item a neck ornament rather than a necklace or an arm ornament rather than a bracelet. This is just a simple gesture attempting to remove generalization and performed, word-function concepts.

Whether or not the result of an idea is wearable is immaterial to me in the initial stage. The concept — which is very often a pure and simple notion about a movement, a rhythm, a rigid pattern, a tactile surface — is processed sometimes two-dimensionally but usually three-dimensionally. In exploration, the idea is worked in materials that have the same or similar properties to what the article might eventually be made in. It is during this development that the idea might become wearable as an object. This is when the problems of function are encountered.

Alternately, the final statement could be an object of fascination — which must be equally as valid. The idea is of prime importance. The wearability of it is secondary. It is not new for items of adornment and fashion to be uncomfortable.

The jewelry should not only enhance the wearer, but should also be a fascinating object in its own right. I see no particular virtue in handmade work that is purely for handmade's sake. If it is necessary for me to use a machine to obtain a particular quality at a particular speed, then it is only honest to the situation to use the machine.

The "purely handmade" mystique is perpetuated by the craftsmen who
do not have the ability to adapt to the times and the advancement
of technology. I could go on making statements of what I think
forever, but the final product would no doubt be of value to one
person only — namely me!

Two armbands.

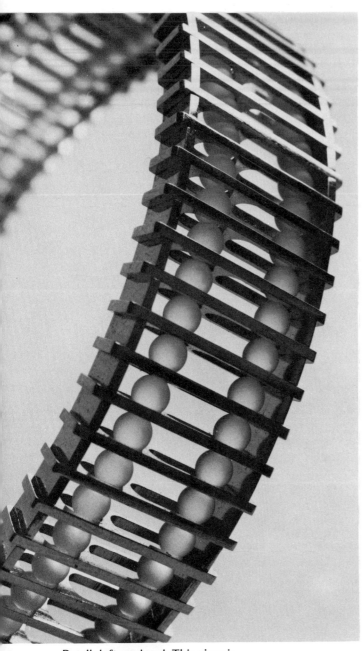

Detail, left armband. This piece is rhodium plated, with precision ground glass balls. The balls are free to move in the tracks created by the holes in each adjacent unit. The units (which were cut out with the aid of a pantograph) are fitted into corresponding slots in the two circular units. The piece is so exact in construction that no soldering was required.

Detail, right armband. Made from silver, titanium, and glass balls. The balls were precision ground and are trapped between the rivet heads and the base plate of titanium. The silver is left matt, and the titanium is its natural gray color. The rivets are of oxidized silver.

32

A pair of titanium, silver, and glass armbands. The base plate is made of 3-millimeter-thick perforated titanium into which silver rivets, made from seamless tube, are forced. Precision-ground glass balls are trapped between the rivet heads and the base plate. Space has been left to allow the balls to move within this trap, thus producing a slight sound and creating subtle tactile and visual quality while being worn. The titanium is heat colored, and the silver has been left white.

Stainless steel spring neck ornament with solid glass balls enclosed in each of the two interlocked springs. The clasp is magnetic. The elasticity of the springs is sufficient to hold the ornament to the body, but is not so strong that it constricts in any way.

Ray Norman
Australia

Ray Norman heads a jewelry and metalsmith studio in connection with Sturt Workshops, Mittagong, New South Wales.

Words work for me only on a very personal level with people I feel close to. I guess that's why I make jewelry. It's like an extension of my voice. The language is so bloody limited — there are so few things you can really say clearly with words. But then, our society is hung up on words, isn't it? And all the words keep going on while other "languages" are virtually ignored. Like, for example, politicians can debate for hours on whether or not to hold a debate. They just cancel themselves out. It's not my thing.

It seems to me that Western man is in almost total conflict with his environment. In our country, we live near aboriginal men who are in total harmony with their natural environment. These people still know how to *feel* — to make use of all their senses. This ability has been educated right out of the rest of us. We've replaced it with "logic," and logic has become our god. We formulate our judgments based upon logic, and then, if anything happens to be left over, we let our emotions and senses enter in. The aboriginal man functions exactly the other way around. And what do we do? We call him a "primitive."

I suppose at least unconsciously I'm at the point of trying to get a bit back in the direction of the aboriginal man — trying to rediscover some of my own instincts and responses.

Perhaps to many people my work appears to be schizophrenic because I don't come on strong with a personal style. I guess there are just too many things I still want to discover to close myself into a stylistic bag. I guess a style is a possibility, but I'm not yet to that point. I sit here in Australia. This is Asia. I can go to the West for my influences, but it would be more geographically natural for me to turn to Japan or China. An Australian-European just doesn't have a cultural background similar to a European or to an Asian. We've only been around on our own continent for about 200 years.

As for jewelry — well, it seems to me that there is only so far you can take a jewel by yourself. You can put into it everything you've got, but it never really becomes a jewel until it becomes a part of someone else. It seems to me that an object never becomes a jewel until it becomes like a nose or an ear to another person.

Sometimes I start my form-building from very rough drawings, but usually I just start from an idea and then let myself and the idea grow together until we understand one another. There is a kind of defining process going on as the object grows into a reality.

Silver to me seems wet, hard, and full of aesthetic qualities. Because of its wetness and hardness, it also has a sort of softness. I like to contrast materials: for example, the dryness of ceramic blended with the wetness of silver. There is no reason why they both can't live together when they relate in a way that I feel is meaningful. I'm into jewelry being more than just something to look at. You have to touch it, feel it, and smell it. It needs a tactile reaction. That's why I sometimes put materials like cow hair with metal. If the contrasting elements work together, then I think one is able to produce a kind of energy within the form.

If one is not technically proficient, then one is nowhere. But immaculate technique by itself is not enough. Techniques are just sort of roads one takes in order to realize something else. If the feeling, emotion, or love isn't there, then the technique is useless because it expresses nothing.

I've tried a lot to do things with my students in order to get them to feel, but it's not easy. Most of the feelings have been buggered out of us by the time we are five. It's not easy to find them again. Our "education" has educated our feelings away. How do you get somebody to find his feelings? Do you shove a pin up his ass and get him to recognize pain as a feeling? We seem to have stopped too much of our capacity to relate emotionally to things. Yes, a school can teach you a technical vocabulary, but it can't teach you the language. The language comes from understanding the whole rather than the parts.

So far, the distant future doesn't exist for me. I can't afford the time to think about it. How do we know what the future holds in store for jewelry? Who knows? The most important thing one can do is just to try and maintain honesty as we proceed into the future.

People talk about freedom. What do I think about freedom? I think most of the talk is crap. I think freedom is in itself just another discipline.

Fabricated 18-carat gold ring with carnelian beads. The beads rotate on their spindles like beads on an abacus.

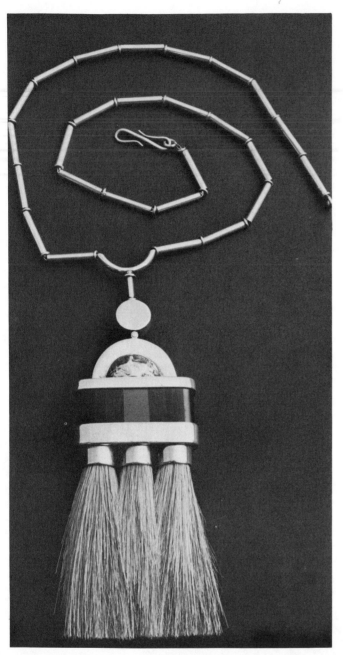

Detail, sterling silver pendant with
cow-tail hair.

Sterling silver pendant with cow-tail
hair, laminated jasper, and petrified
wood. The silver hanging mechanism allows the pendant to swivel.
Cow-tail hairs were first attached to
a piece of wire, then pulled up into
the silver tubes and cemented in
place.

Native "Mittagong" porcelain pendants with sterling silver hanging mechanisms. Screw-heads, tubes, and even watch gears were used to texture the ceramic. The hanging mechanism was made so that it is interchangeable with several pendants. Ray's idea was to produce inexpensive pendant forms that could be interchanged with the same collar.

Ring of fabricated sterling silver 18-carat gold, laminated jasper, and petrified wood. The stone and wood pieces were laminated with epoxy and then cut and polished before being set.

Regine Juhls
Norway

Regine Juhls lives and works far above the Arctic Circle in Norwegian Lapland. Obviously, time has quite another meaning for Regine than for most of the rest of us. In the summer, Regine's life is filled with perpetual daylight; in the winter, with perpetual darkness.

Yes, I'm a being who I guess looks at everything I see from an aesthetic point of view. But the beauty I see is not just the self-evident beauty one sees in great hunks of nature. No, I am able to find beauty everywhere. Even in a street gutter.

I think that my need to create comes from a need to build a whole world on another planet — a kind of place which is a compensation for the real world I've been born into, where it is next to impossible to be accepted as a whole. Too much of our everyday life avoids the whole.

Even if I'm a bad handworker — in every sense impractical — I never do simple forms. I seem to do myself the inconvenience of putting my jewelry and sculptural forms together by small details requiring endless patience.

My work table is always filled with silver pieces, bones, shells, self-dried mushrooms, bark, roots, and unusual stones which I've found lying around on the tundra. One detail can take me several months of work. If I were to write, I guess I would be one of those authors that never lost his inspiration during the process of putting together 1,000 sides of a book. The character I am describing has to be exposed in all its complications; it has to be illuminated from all sides. Nothing should be excluded in trying to capture an acceptable whole. I think I associate best with metal just because it offers these technical difficulties.

My best work time is the night, no matter if it's summer or winter. When I'm depressed, my work represents a kind of therapy. I think it's important to create something. The only problem is the time — to get the time to last. Ideas come to me continually, probably because my surroundings make such a deep impression upon me. I feel there are forms lying, standing, and floating everywhere. I'd like to help them along. Help them forward from their accidental state. Help to develop them into accomplished entireties. Just watch, for example, what can happen only when you spill coffee onto a shiny table surface.

Fabricated form in silver, 16 centimeters high.

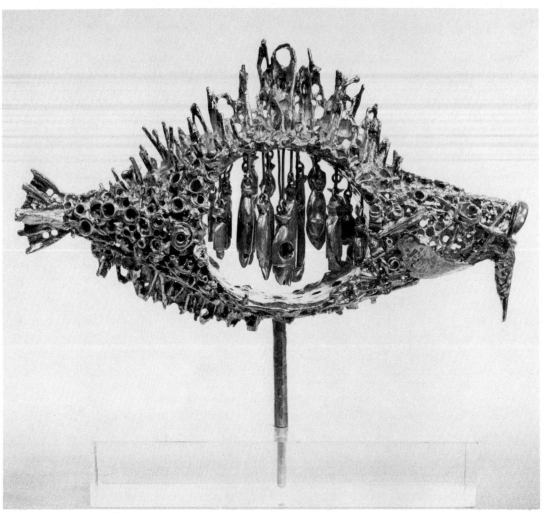

Fabricated "motherfish" in silver, 17 centimeters long. The story behind this piece is that Regine received a commission to create an award for a summer fishing festival in a small northern Norwegian village. To begin research for the form, Regine went out fishing with a rod and reel and caught herself a cod in order to study its personality. As the form developed, she grew so attached to it that she decided to keep it herself, and had to beg the festival committee to find another silversmith to create the award.

"Motherfish," second view. The forms inside the fish move independently, and Regine considers them "fish children."

40

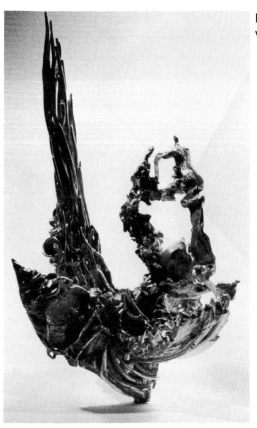

Fabricated form in silver, second view.

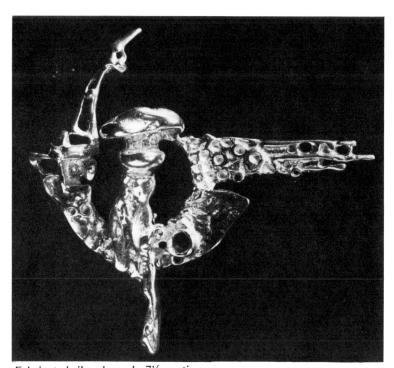

Fabricated silver brooch, 7½ centi-meters long.

Fabricated silver brooch, 19 centi-meters long. *Regine Juhls.*

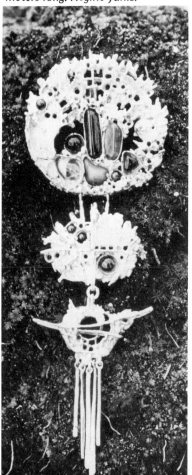

Three Japanese Artists

Fabricated ring. *Yasuki Hiramatsu.*

Three 18-carat gold rings. *Yasuki Hiramatsu*, Japan.

9-carat white gold ring. *Yasuki Hiramatsu.*

43

Fabricated brooch. *Yasuki Hiramatsu.*

Silver pin with pearl. *Eugene Pijanowski.*

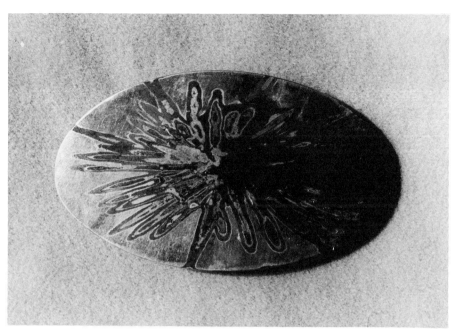

Pin. *Eugene Pijanowski.* The artist uses the Japanese technique "mokume-nagashi," or wood-graining. The piece is made from silver, gold, and "shakudo," a special alloy from pure gold and copper, which produces a black metal.

Fabricated silver ring with rutilated quartz. *Eugene Pijanowski.*

Pin. *Eugene Pijanowski,* Japan. Materials include silver, brass, and "shakudo."

45

Ring. *Yasuki Hiramatsu.*

Ring. *Yasuki Hiramatsu.*

14-carat gold, partly oxidized pin
with pearls. *Hiroko Sato
Pijanowski,* Japan.

Back view, fabricated silver
bracelet. *Eugene Pijanowski.*

Front view, fabricated silver
bracelet. *Eugene Pijanowski.*

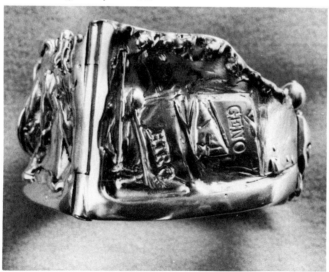

Pendant of silver with agate. *Hiroko Sato Pijanowski.*

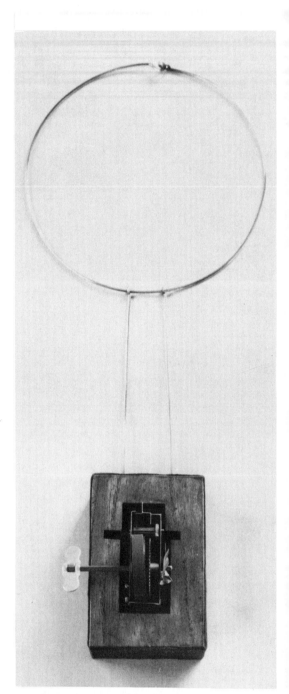

Moving pendant in silver, wood, leather, and zircon. *Hiroko Sato Pijanowski.*

Pendant of silver, agate, and smoky
quartz. *Hiroko Sato Pijanowski.*

Pendant of silver, agate, and smoky
quartz. *Hiroko Sato Pijanowski.*

Marci Zelmanoff
United States

Marci Zelmanoff has described herself both as an "ex-radical," and as "really a nice Jewish girl at heart (ha)." When the radical Marci is showing her colors, she will say things like: "Artists are on about the same level as niggers and women — each group allowed a few who make it big, with the rest treated like dirt." But when Marci's opposite side is in the forefront, she grows reflective, even sentimental, and worries (a little) about whether her manner of expressing herself is perhaps too "gutsy."

Marci not only wraps and knots fine silver wire, but she has recently started to combine electroforming, casting, and forging within hand fabrication. She has this to say about herself and her work.

My new work is much different, more bold, but still as frantic — though hard to describe. It's creepy work, and it's hanging me up. I'm somewhere in the middle of arrogantly saying that my work speaks for itself and humbly admitting that I don't really know what the devil I'm doing. I've been thinking about it for a while and honestly don't know what to say. I find it a psychological barrier to commit my "soul" to paper, since paper isn't my thing. All I can say is I want to make gutsy jewelry — so what? Craft books haven't turned me on much, maybe because I haven't been in any before (ha) or maybe because I feel that most metalsmiths are rigid — the nature of the material makes them that way.

It's sort of like this: when someone tells you to relax, it can make you five times as uptight. And when I'm called upon to be "meaningful" . . . well, all of a sudden I find myself sitting in front of the mirror putting on makeup.

Otherwise, things are a bit encouraging. I am selling small stuff like rings and belt buckles — not in great quantities, but enough to pay silver bills and car insurance (but not yet the rent). Actually, I'm quite busy, possibly too busy getting ready for shows and turning out "sellies" to put myself on a soul-searching level. Also, it seems that I'm not as interested in me and my goals and my problems as I was a year ago — what a relief!

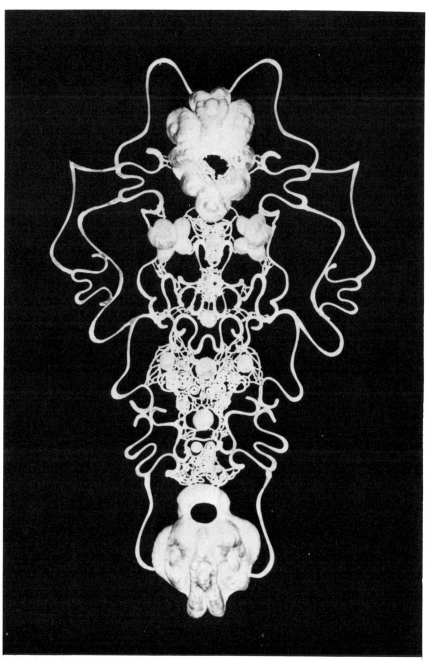

Cast, forged, chased, and wrapped
fine and sterling silver.

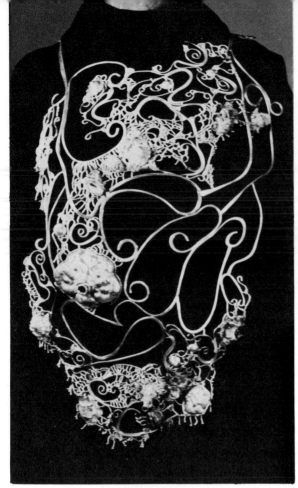

"Chestpiece." Cast, formed, chased, and wrapped fine and sterling silver. 16 x 22 x 6 inches.

"Beyond Jewelry." Marci says this is a hanging or a neckpiece for someone 6 feet 5 inches tall. It is forged, chased sterling, and wrapped fine silver wire.

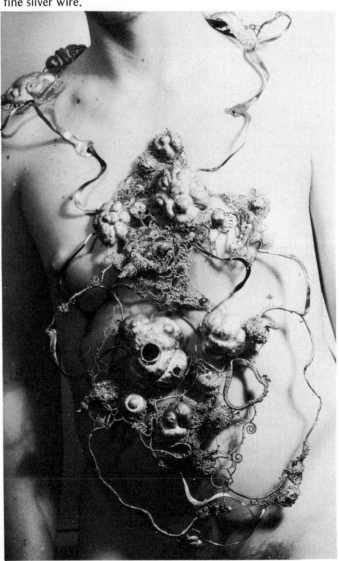

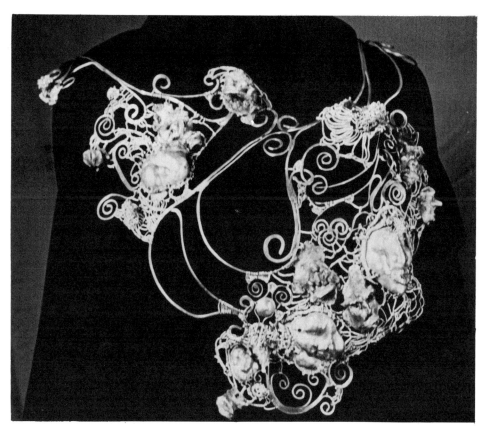

"Form with Faces." Front view.

"Form with Faces," detail.

53

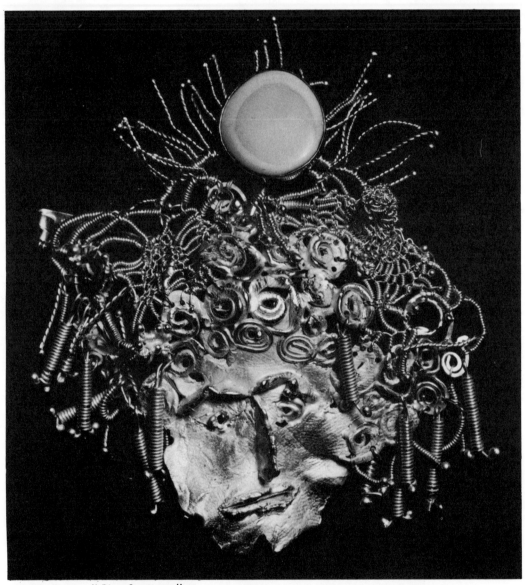

"Lady Doctor." Pin of cast sterling
with wrapped wire and whale
ivory. 3 inches across.

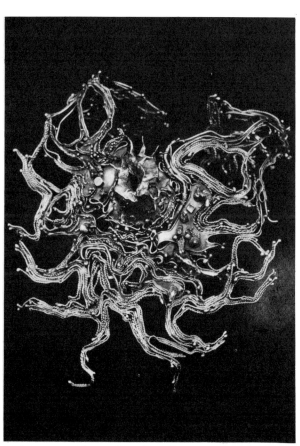

Neckpiece in fine and sterling silver.
Cast, electroformed, and fabricated.
12 x 14 x 6 inches.

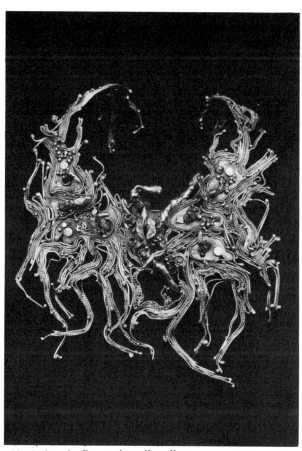

Neckpiece in fine and sterling silver.
Cast, electroformed, and fabricated.
12 x 6 x 6 inches.

Arline Fisch

United States

Many months ago, Arline Fisch became the first guru or sounding board off of which I bounced the embryo idea for this book. Arline drove down from Copenhagen to visit me on the whimsical Danish island of Fyn, where I was then living. We sat knocking ideas about and desperately trying to define a responsible future path for jewelry publishing. What seemed clear to us both was that the future had to lie somewhere other than where the past had been. I proposed the unpolished idea for this book, and Arline not only confirmed the idea but added ideas of her own. Her positive response not only cleared my head but also helped to lift my sails. But this is, of course, typical for Arline Fisch — always looking around corners, seldom stagnant, and quick to add a measure of encouragement to positive energy.

Arline is no stranger to a suitcase or to the hum of wheels or wings. She has a nose for people. Needless to say, the many personal contacts resulting from her world travels eventually became an invaluable starting point from which this book grew.

In her own work, Arline not only knits, weaves, and wraps fine silver wire, but she also mounts feathers and forms metal. Her garmentlike forms often contain surprising combinations of materials as well as techniques.

I am always willing to share ideas, observations, thoughts, techniques, et cetera — but my guts are strictly my own. I share Ruth Radakovich's feeling that the public does not have a right to buy, sell, or own the artist along with his art. I say this, not out of any sense of selfishness, but only because most of us have a desperate need for privacy in our personal lives if we are to work with any kind of intensity and integrity. Dealers, museums, and clients alike tend to deal with the person only as an extension of the commodity of his art. Nobody likes to feel like a bag of groceries to be marketed and consumed, no matter how elevated the level may sound. And that goes for people who write books, too! What I share with readers through a book is my work and what I think about my work — all else remains my private domain.

I have often thought that it must be incredibly difficult to be a jeweler and a male, because it means that one is almost always designing and making objects for other people. I suppose that is, in fact, the way that most jewelers work. Somewhat abstractly, and without a close personal relationship with the objects they create. For me, that approach has become increasingly uninspiring, if not impossible. I relate very closely to the jewelry I make. I really make it for myself, and never consider a piece finished until I have worn it at least once in public. The wearing in public is particularly important to me because I think it is only in that situation that a piece of jewelry can be evaluated and appreciated fully. (What joy is there in designing pieces to sit in bank vaults? Better a small pouch of diamonds for the vault and a piece of jewelry for the lady!) Personal adornments should only be complete when they are on a person. They need the structure and the movement of the human form to realize their total effect. And the effect — that is the most important aspect of all. Just as adornments are used ritualistically to add beauty and wonder to important personages (and not only in primitive cultures — consider the regalia of the Christian religions!), so contemporary jewelry should enhance and besplendor individuals who wish to be noticed as being someone special. This motivation exists in many people who express their personalities in the way they adorn themselves with clothing and jewelry. If only one other person relates to a piece, then I consider it a success because it means that the strong character I try to give to my work is speaking to another personality and they are augmenting each other — a highly stimulating event.

Looking at my recent work objectively (which I do only rarely), I can see that things have assumed a quite ritualistic tone. The scale of individual ornaments, the use of beads and feathers, of faces and wings, all relate to the cultures whose work I have studied in great detail: pre-Columbian Peru and Mexico, Egypt, Africa, Eskimo, and American Indian. This has been a rather unconscious development which has been growing for the past several years, and I am not unhappy with the direction now that I see it more clearly. It seems to fit logically with my own needs for humanistic and imagistic forms as well as for larger-scale effects which are still comfortable to, and compatible with, the human form. It also somehow is an appropriate direction for the times, or so it seems to me at the moment.

Knitted 18-carat gold brooch with cultured pearls.

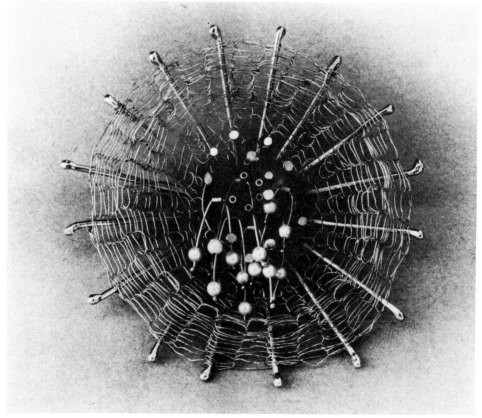

Necklace. Woven sheet sterling and fine silver wire. The sheet sterling was first milled until flexible enough for weaving. The weaving was done flat and the form was bent afterward. The weave is twill. The domestic bird feathers are held in place by extra lengths of fine silver weft that was coiled around the feather shafts. The warp is sheet sterling.

Detail, woven necklace

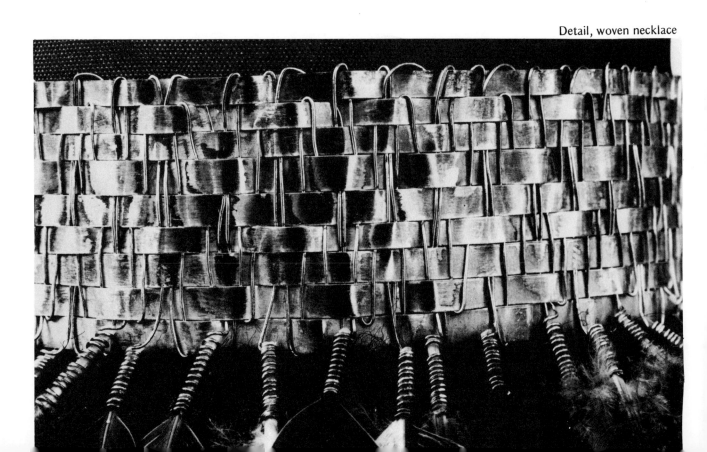

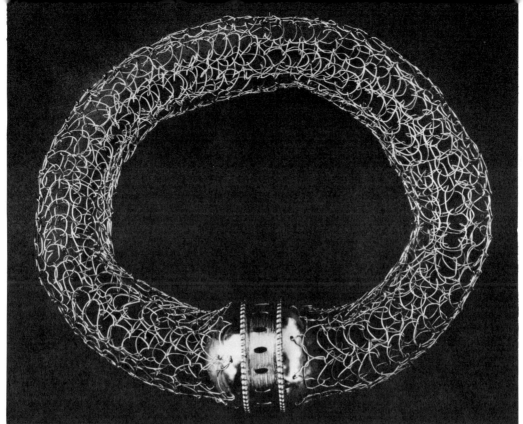

Knitted fine silver necklace with sterling clasp. The process, "spool knitting," was done over a plastic ring, using 30-gauge fine silver wire.

Detail, knitted fine silver necklace. Clasp ball is worn in front. The ball clasp opens by twisting, and is made in two halves.

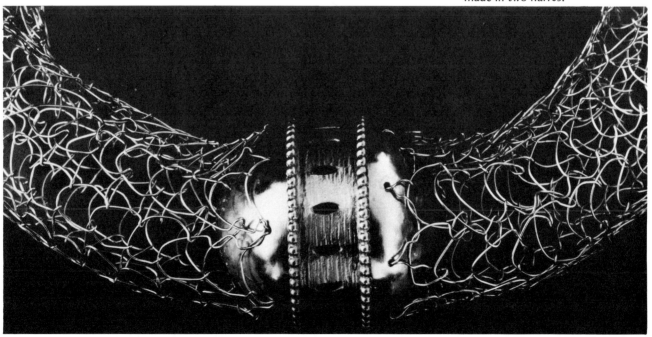

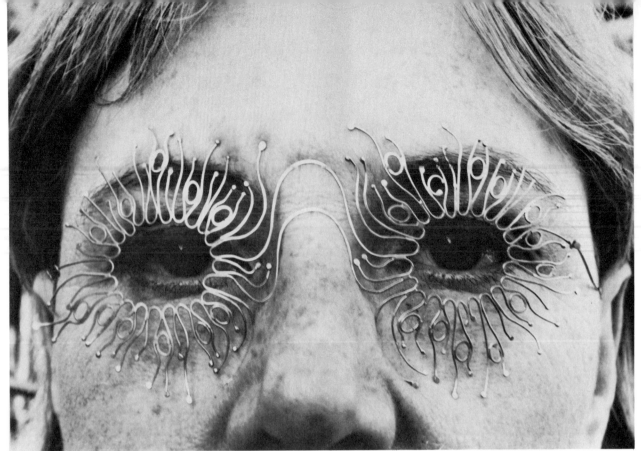

Fabricated 18-carat gold glasses for
people who wear contacts.

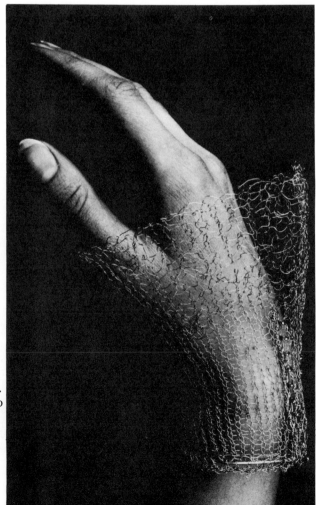

18-carat gold knitted cuff. This
form was knitted with ordinary
knitting needles of 2 different sizes.
It was knitted flat, and then bent to
form. The edges were finished by
adding a row of crocheted wire.

Silver collar. Braided and twined
fine silver wire with silver dangles.

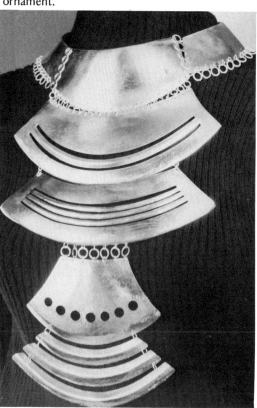

Fabricated sterling silver chest
ornament.

"The Devil Himself." Chased silver pendant.

"Moroccan Memory." Silver and amber necklace.

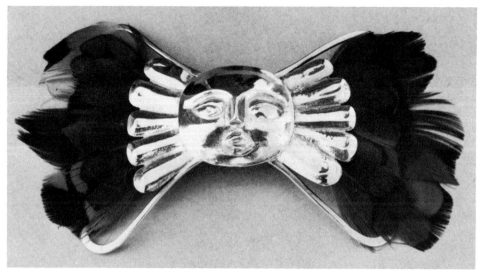

Chased 18-carat gold brooch with pheasant feathers. Feathers are held in place by individual concealed tubes.

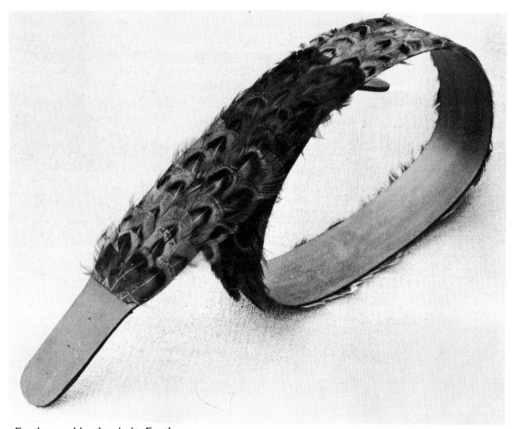

Feather and leather belt. Feathers were first individually cemented to a textile backing and the backing was then contact-cemented onto leather.

Mary Lee Hu
United States

Although her medium is jewelry, Mary Lee Hu is also a student of both the Chinese language and Chinese musical instruments. Recently she has been living, traveling, and researching in southeast Asia, particularly Taiwan.

As for my work, I limit myself to using only wire with the occasional addition of a stone bead or a thin silver sheet. I became interested in the use of wire in 1966 while studying macramé. After using the wire for macramé in several pieces, I decided I was fighting the basic characteristics of the wire — its stiffness and its ability to be bent smoothly and evenly, once only. So then I started wrapping one wire around another wire, or even around another group of wires, and then combining these wires in various ways. Basket weaving seemed a well-suited technique to use in gaining larger, lightweight forms.

I consider wire ends very important. If they can be used for a decorative effect, then I try to do so. Otherwise, they should be completely hidden from view. The process of melting these ends to form balls presented itself as an ideal way of utilizing the ends. The most important factor in my technique is that I use fine, rather than sterling, silver. The bright, light color, the extreme softness, and the ease of handling, as well as the possibility of melting the ends quickly and evenly without the mess and bother of a flux, were all made possible by this choice of wire. I use sterling only for the core of pieces when rigidity is needed. Recently, I have been using enameled electrical wire for its color. It cannot, however, stand the heat of the torch.

My direction has been divided fairly evenly between jewelry and small insects or animals which are not designed to be worn. Lately, however, this division is breaking down: some of my creatures have been slowly creeping into my jewelry. I have limited myself to making pieces for my own enjoyment and have eliminated those processes of jewelry making which I did not find enjoyable — namely soldering, filing, buffing, and polishing. I like the fact that all of my steps are clearly visible within the finished form and that I need only a minimum of equipment — the wire, my fingers, fingernails, and, occasionally, a pair of pliers.

Headpiece.

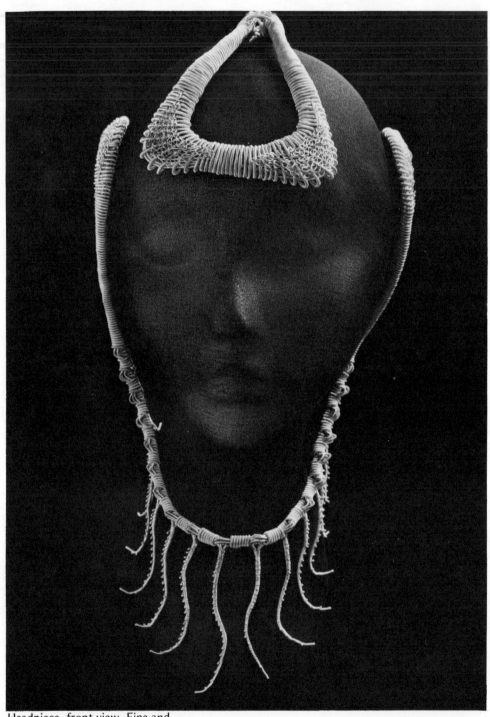

Headpiece, front view. Fine and
sterling silver wire.

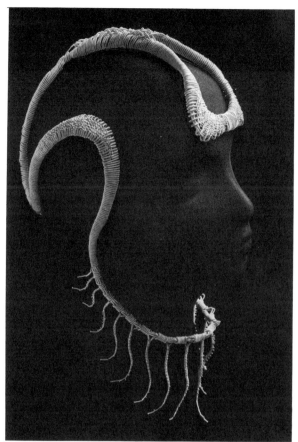

Headpiece, side view.

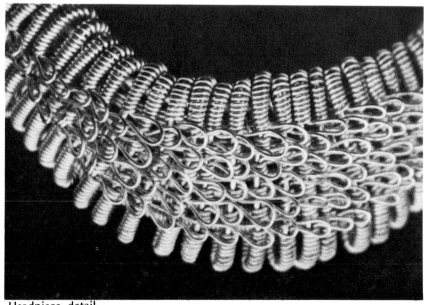

Headpiece, detail.

Headpiece, front view.

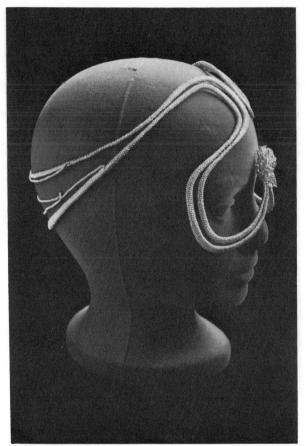

Headpiece, side view.

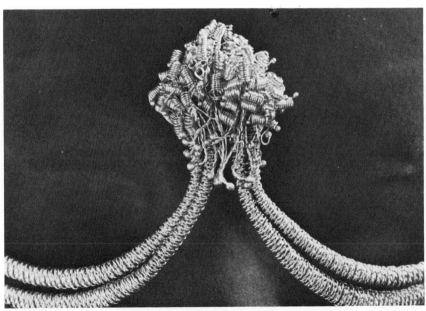

Headpiece, forehead detail.

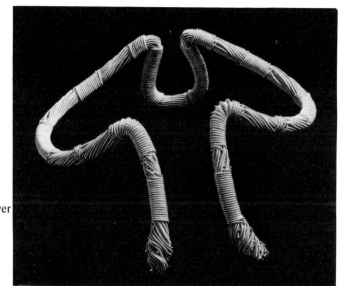

Neckpiece. Fine and sterling silver wire.

Neckpiece, of fine and sterling silver wire with fine gold and enameled nickel alloy.

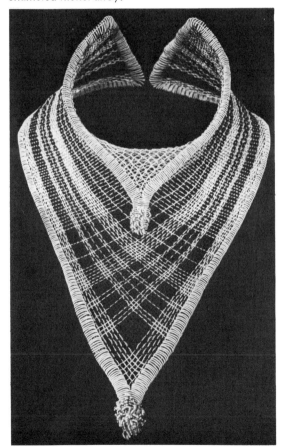

Neckpiece, detail.

Wann-hong Liu
Republic of China

Wann-hong Liu is both a private craftsman and a research associate at the National Palace Museum in Taipei, Taiwan. Much of his "official" work is devoted to the study of the Shang Bronzes — not only finding out how they were made but also restoring and attempting to reproduce them with the same techniques.

Wann-hong has often found an application for his research in his own work. He expresses much of his fantasy through gold and silver wire, using the material somewhat like macramé, by twisting, winding, knotting, and braiding it into form.

As for jewelry making, I always say that I am a free ideal, and a patient craftsman. I like to construct free-form and sculptural-form jewelry with rich designs, using all kinds of materials and time-consuming techniques.

Sculptural bracelet. Made from 18-, 20-, and 22-gauge sterling silver wire that was twisted, bent, wound, and braided.

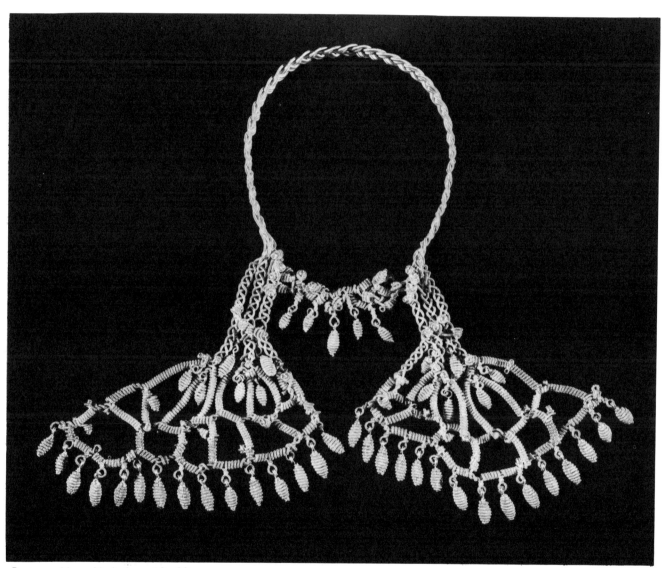

Party necklace. Made from 18-, 20-,
and 22-gauge sterling silver wire
that was twisted, bent, wound, and
braided.

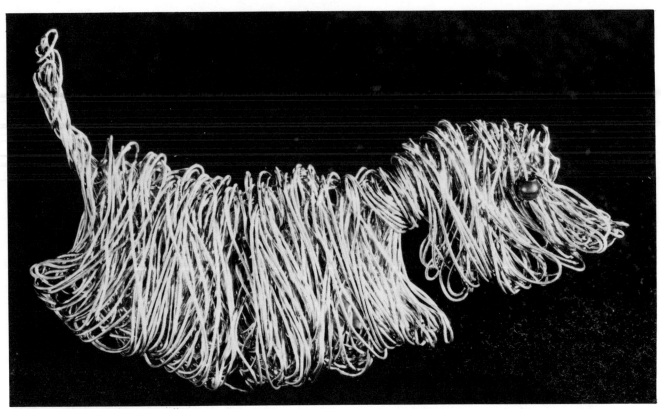

Dog pin. Made of 18-gauge sterling
silver wire that was free-wrapped.

Party necklace.

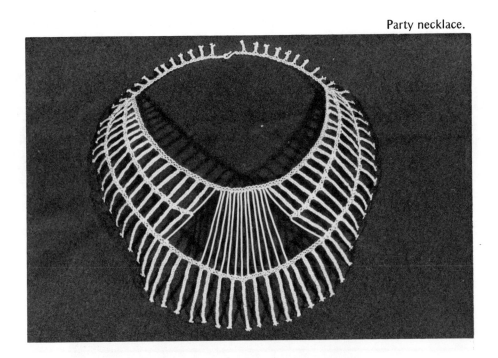

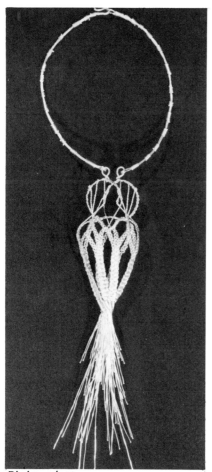

Bird pendant.

Sculptural pendant.

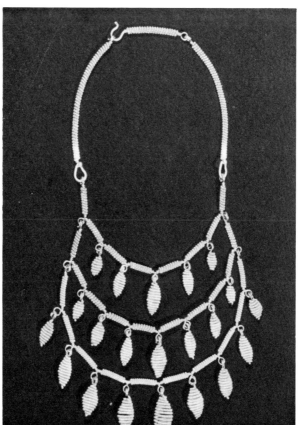

Party necklace.

Edward Koelling
and Mary Lou Higgins
United States

In the summer of 1971, Ed and Mary Lou worked together — sometimes fifteen hours a day — to realize a lifetime wish. They built their own house, which was not at all unlike a sculptural extension of their craft forms — a situation where the fantasy for jewelry form actually grew so large that Ed and Mary Lou were able to move inside. The house ended up so unlike other houses that before they had even dirtied the carpet they were entertaining tourists. Mary Lou says they don't really mind the tourists, except that they consume so much time.

Edward Koelling

The excitement, mystique, richness, poorness, barrenness, complexity, and simplicity of man in his movements and involvements are the subjects of my jewelry. Translated into the small size of pendants and rings, they gain a power and relationship with the wearer. The jewelry is created to have thought-provoking periods while it is being worn and seen. I also hope that whoever wears my jewelry will be involved personally with it and involved privately in an art form.

I find, at this moment, that the process of casting and assembling best expresses my designs and forms — and these in turn express my emotions, feelings, attitudes, and reactions. My themes are feedbacks of our news and also feedbacks from the quiet involvement of very introverted students that are being mutilated by the overly extroverted emotional students I work with. Being involved with today's college students compels the contemporary artist to scream out his feelings. Ironically, I feel that small sculptural forms in jewelry can do my best screaming.

"All That Is Rich Is Not Man."
Pendant cast in silver with sapphires
and mink-tail trim.

"Ride a Gold Horse to a Cock
Dream." Gold-plated cast ring.

"Land Ho — Pull in Your Wheels."
Gold-plated cast ring.

"Last Place." Gold-plated cast ring.

Mary Lou Higgins

I have evolved through the conventional type of jewelry. After metal work, I began to lean toward the fiber-fabric area. My first pieces were a type of crocheted necklace, but then my forms began to increase across the chest and down the back. They grew from necklaces into full chest and back forms. As they grew, my use of techniques and materials also grew. They grew from crocheting into macramé, and from traditional fiber into using beads, feathers, fur, blocks of teak, and even fabrics and hair.

From this point, the arms began to play a part in my forms. And then, as my awareness of the arms grew, my concepts also grew to include sculptural shoulder bags or forms hanging below the arms. My forms have been "additive" items to enhance, decorate, or design around or across another form — namely, the human body. But is adding a valid device or art form? Is the item that is under the jewelry form detracting? Is it ruining the whole concept, the concept of the human body?

As a result of asking myself these questions, I am now creating forms that I feel are "jewelry art forms" in a very broad sense of the term. They are complete and independent forms. The wearer slips into the creation and becomes a complete art form within himself. Thus today each soft sculptural form that I create to be worn is a complete entity — it needs nothing except a very warm, alive human being to bring its form into context with its environment.

And when I say this, I am not talking about conventional garments. I am not involved in seams, bias, hems, et cetera. I am involved in soft sculptural forms that flow and move around the human body. The body is the showcase for the form. The environment in which the form is worn is the gallery.

I feel that this type of sculptural body experience is very free and exciting to the wearer. The complete form seems to bring to the wearer a sensuous excitement and awareness of vitality that had not before been experienced. Yet, at the same time, the sculptural body forms relax the physical form and give it back its natural, animal grace. I intend to pursue this direction much more.

Crocheted bag. Lynx fur, beads,
feathers, and acrilon fiber.

Woven coat of fiber and fur.

Macramé form in leather, beads, and teak.

Macramé and crocheted necklace in
mohair and lynx fur.

Nilda Getty
Argentina

Nilda Getty works with both fabric and metal, combining both materials in the same piece and often achieving jewelry form which is garmentlike in character. Recently she has been teaching at Colorado State University. Her American contacts have prompted her to organize craft and intellectual exchanges between North, Central, and South American craftsmen in order to bring these craftsmen closer together. About her work, and her craft, Nilda says this.

A challenge, always appealing to the intellectual sovereignty of man's mind: this is what the subject means to me when a definition, description, or reference needs to be made about my work or about crafts.

I have always believed that crafts should be a way of communicating individual philosophies of the times. Commentaries and involvement with actual events becomes an essential, and many times crucial, basis of the creation.

This was genuine in early times when the crafted objects were mostly considered offerings or were attributed with some magic powers. As civilization developed, art remained true to its beginnings, but crafts became identified with the utilitarian, with the exception of ornaments, which remained akin to the original idea but lacked its forceful meaning.

Whether an ornament is functional or ornamental, secular or religious, formal or spontaneous, "freedom" will emerge from the conceptual creation rather than from its assignment. Thus today, when the machine can take care of our material needs, I feel it is necessary for crafts to free themselves and become once more a plastic expression of our intellect. Art and craft ideas merge into a more unified concept, lending each other support; and a more meaningful manifestation is taking place yielding evidence of the relevance of both as intense translation of individual and social concepts.

The character of my pieces does not reside solely in their aesthetic value, but also in what they communicate. Hidden parts — photographs, stones, bones, shells, feathers — all contribute to give them a more complete intrinsic meaning only recognizable by another believer. Concern for human significance is advocated by form and essence sublimated through expressive quality of line communicating directly to the emotion, where the transcendental resides.

This does not mean disregard for intellectual nobility. On the contrary, intellect is the best tool we have to help interpret those manifestations. Our mistake is to let it overpower the inner reality of man. With McLuhan, I believe in a complete reevaluation of our principles and life; when we conquer this, meaning will become closer to primitive cultures. Ignorance and fear will be replaced by a deeper understanding of the nature of man and a higher level of symbolic realm.

As far as the ritual of "pieces for the human body," I believe both in a totality and in a duality. Totality, because it is very important for me that the art work stand on its own; duality because when it is worn, it should become a new totality together with the person wearing it. It is then that the difficulties arise. The maker and the wearer should share beliefs, or the discrepancy will reveal itself. The craftsman's need to depart from the materialistic world into a spiritual and sometimes mystical sphere requires a counterpart attitude and awareness by the other person involved in order to communicate the embodied mood and the implied meaning.

"Phoenix II." Breast pendant in sterling and 18-carat gold. 17 inches long.

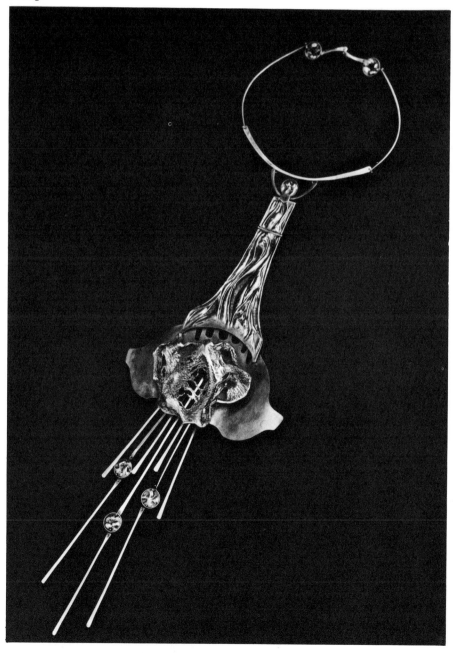

"Izanagi." Body environment in sterling silver.

"Izanagi," side view.

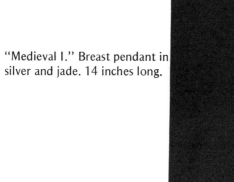

"Medieval I." Breast pendant in silver and jade. 14 inches long.

"Pluie." Garment with silverwork. Metal vibrates and tinkles gently as the garment is worn.

"Pluie," detail of silverwork side piece.

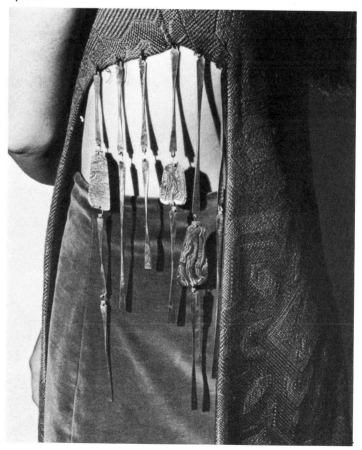

"Artemis." Hip-leg ornament container. Sterling silver and fur.

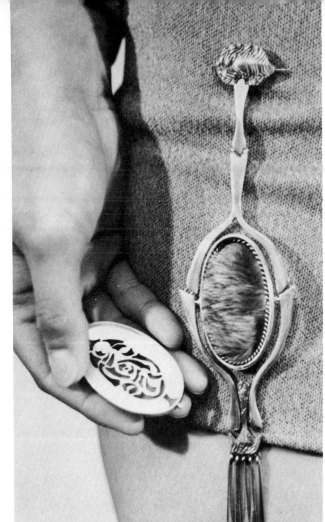

"Artemis," detail of open container.

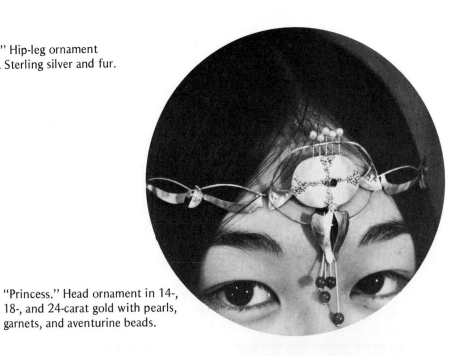

"Princess." Head ornament in 14-, 18-, and 24-carat gold with pearls, garnets, and aventurine beads.

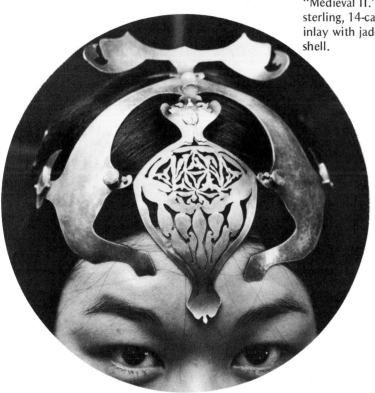

"Medieval II." Head ornament in sterling, 14-carat gold, and brass inlay with jade, moonstone, and shell.

"Medieval II," second view. Front center piece can be removed to change composition.

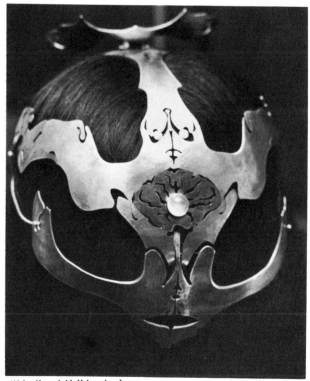

"Medieval II," back view.

Richard Mafong and Jon Riis
United States

"Everybody by now ought to be a bit tired of all the crap that artists drum up in order to explain their work." So says Jon Riis, with the blessing of Richard Mafong.

Richard works in metal, and Jon is a weaver. The two craftsmen work together, combining their talents and their two different technical disciplines within single pieces of jewelry. Jon says that it has been "extremely enjoyable for both Richard and me to work together, but at the same time, it has forced us to face and overcome the difficult problem of combining two very different disciplines, and two very different personalities." Jon feels that working together "not only speeds up the process and the execution of a piece, but it also provides maximum technical possibilities."

"Ceremonial Vest." Woven from linen warp with inlaid tapestry and pile technique. Weft includes wool, alpaca, Indian Muga silk, cotton, and gold metallic threads. Added woven elements are gold-plated brass wire around the silk tassels at the neck. The brass coat-hanger stand is included with the piece.

Brooch with weaving and metal-work. Planished brass with backing of woven fabric. Fabric was woven with "fine tapestry" technique with a linen warp and silk and metallic gold thread weft. Pheasant feathers and white glass beads are added.

Louise Todd

United States

Louise Todd and I have exchanged an incredible volume of correspondence during the building of this book. Among many subjects, we've been exchanging ideas and absurdities on how to build a crafts curriculum with a real potential to avoid stagnancy. Louise has experimented successfully with subjects that are upsetting to tradition.

Louise is a textile artist, but her forms often grow into body adornment. She views body adornment from a perspective quite unlike that of a metalsmith. Louise sees form structure, and she often sees it in terms of close-up, almost microscopic enlargement.

When she expresses her feelings verbally, Louise often writes in great gusts, filling not only the paper but the margins and even the envelope. And while this verbal energy is being unleashed, she is changing unconsciously from one pen to another, and sometimes even adding sentences in pencil, as if to say, "Damn these writing instruments!"

Although I work with threads in many areas, I find myself returning again and again to body adornment. Partly, I think, because I thoroughly enjoy clothes, and I often relish the fun I have because of them. Sometimes they are even the initiation of the fun.

Every single thread begins to assume a life of its own when the body starts to move. This is my fascination — the way the body moves and the way the threads act and react to it. I like a minimal organization, so lots of different patterns and motions can occur. When I discovered the fiber optics it was like magic. Suddenly, here were fibers that could surprise you by a myriad of tiny lights. I remember the first time I turned off all the lights, put on my veil of fiber optics, and gasped: "Incredible!" Like it was being in the midst of the stars.

In the summer of 1971, when I was teaching at Penland, North Carolina, I involved the craftsmen in a project where they were asked to weave "change," or in other words, a woven form not to be in any way static — a form that, when woven by someone else, had the possibility of assuming a myriad of identities. It meant the need of many flexible elements. I also wanted something woven for a man — often neglected in clothing nowadays. Part of the project idea was also to see if an artist could relinquish self. In other words, when an object was completed and the process evolved, could the artist relinquish the object completely, feeling no sense of "preciousness," so that the piece could then assume its own life? Another year, we involved ourselves in a project to weave sound. Yes, I do like people to think, and to accept challenge.

Face veil. Fiber and nylon fishing
yarn. Crown is wrapped with linen.

Head covering. Knotted fishing
fiber and stoneware beads.

Body covering. Knotted fishing
fiber and porcelain beads.

91

Body covering in linked aluminum with hood. *Jakobine Hobbs,* United States.

"Fringed Fantasy." Body covering in dyed rooster feathers, satin, canvas, velvet, and velour. *Joan Ann Jablow*, United States.

93

Rita Shumaker

United States

I make things: paintings, prints, pot roasts, havoc, drawings, hangings, jewelry, pastry, and love. It is my nature. My work changes because I change. Through my work, I express nonverbal responses to my world — a world filled with color, texture, and shapes that give me wonder, awe, and joy. If another person finds meaning in my work, it is because we share the tangible world, a physiology, and, if Carl Jung is correct, an intangible world of unconscious symbols that make our human responses similar.

Presently, the forms my pieces take grow from inside out — in other words, they spring from the ground of the unconscious where reactions to the environment are stored. Often the symbols appear to be cryptograms that set up multilevel vibrations in the viewer. The strongest of these are archetypes, but this is only my theory. My work is an expression of self — self in the Greek sense of "psyche" — and as such, it mirrors my own human condition.

My problems with exhibitions, marketing, galleries, and commissions continue to be similar to those of others. There is never enough time. I very often build form from weaving, and the processes are so slow and the demands so great that I am always three years behind in my sketchbooks. The natural evolution of my work is therefore impeded by the pragmatics of professionalism. But I believe the solution is within my control. I must simply focus myself back into the growth of my work and allow exhibition and similar demands to remain on the periphery. When working only toward markets and the like, I find that I must always keep myself on guard against "outside" motivation. Without a full commitment of self to the piece, an artistic statement can become merely facile.

As human beings, we share impenetrable depths of psychic awareness, multilevels of cognitive and sensate experience. We are surrounded by form, color, motion, texture, and structure. We experience — both instinctively and intuitively — wonder and awe, as well as despair and joy, with the recognition of the phenomena of our world. Our journey of discovery is the quest for the Grail. Art is but an attempt to share the discoveries of that quest.

I very much like the concept of risk and change — of evolution and growth. After all, life itself is a gamble, and *real* living always involves risk. All of the timeworn adages proclaim the necessity of risk:

Risk pain to have love.
Risk sorrow to have joy.
Risk loss to know gain.
Risk failure to know discovery.
Risk censure to know honesty.

These are concepts which must concern us all if we are to survive.

What I (maybe many of us) really need to do is to back off and spend a long, unstructured, nondirected period in the studio, just painting, feeling around with fibers, metal, and whatever — I guess a kind of *Gestalt.* The past six months have all been too directed — too preplanned and overcommitted. It reads like a convincing argument to go off into the wood — so tally ho! I believe I will.

94

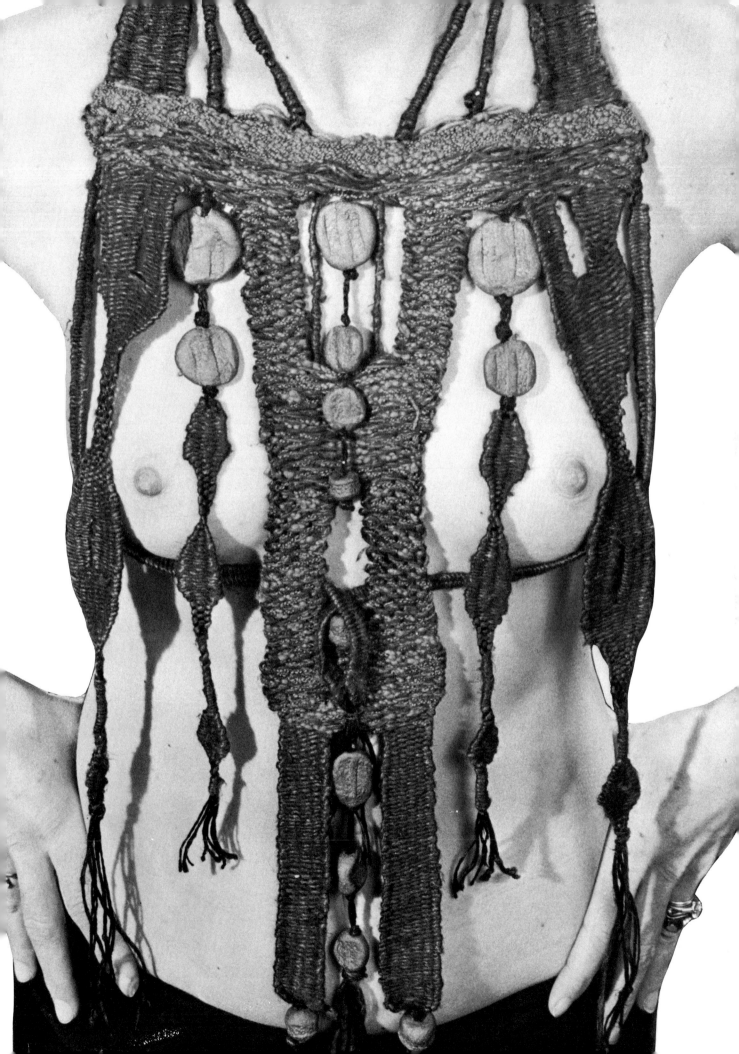

Headdress. Hand-dyed wool with
nylon. Woven with double-weave
tube technique. Other parts wrapped
and knotted.

Knotted and woven breastplate
with feathers and Raku beads.
Fibers include linen and wool.

Woven collar in mohair and wool
with stoneware beads.

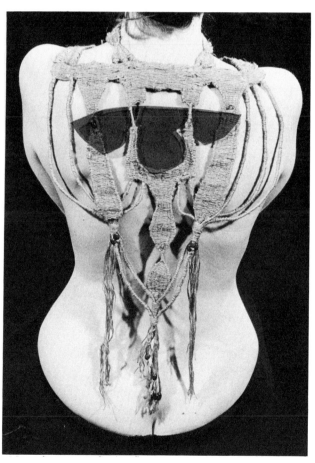

Tapestry-woven and wrapped
breastplate with plexiglass insert
and wooden beads.

Marita Kulvik
Finland

After completing her jewelry education, Marita began working as an industrial jewelry designer for one of the two blueblood firms in Finland. After about three years of being industrially jockeyed — all the way from designer, to salesgirl, to gift wrapper, to translator, to window decorator — she did a refueling job and switched to red-blooded handwork.

Although the bluebloods looked upon the switch as a demotion, her move proved no less than a complete overhaul, topped off with a recharged creative battery. Marita began moving out in many directions — knotting, crocheting, and braiding body forms in hemp, sisal, nylon, and rawhide; hand-fabricating silver, brass, and copper onto leather belts, handbags, and vest forms; and even producing combinations of fur, leather, ceramic, and fiber that appeared on forms for the breast, the back, the face, the head, and wherever else she felt it could work artistically in good function.

And Marita has done even more. She's been a helpmate in patching this book together, sometimes patching its author together, translating our German, Swedish, Norwegian, and Finnish contributors into English, and often even translating authorly chaos into English.

I have a very strong feeling for metal, yet I sometimes object to the way the material dictates a working procedure. Sometimes it's pleasant just to relax while you work and to eliminate the use of a lot of tools and technical awareness. Fibers can do this — they can present a whole alternative way of working. I've therefore found a way of balancing out my personality demands by using both metal and fibers. And then, too, I like working with color. By coloring my own fibers, I can reach a spectrum of color which would be otherwise impossible when working directly on metal. For my own tastes, metal satisfies my eyes and my touch when it has a defined form precise in all its corners and roundings. Fibers, on the other hand, seem to be at home with endless subtlety.

When I work, I need to get completely involved in what I'm doing. Perhaps this is why I prefer working in the night — there are fewer distractions. Many people don't seem to understand what this kind of total work involvement is all about. To them, it looks like only the hands are busy, but that's only half of it. My head clears while I'm working. It's a time when my ideas and impressions are putting themselves together with my hands.

I think jewelry is something which belongs *with* the body. Jewelry is not just another way of expressing an idea! The reality of the human body is implicit in jewelry. I get irritated with craftsmen who cry out, "Long live the idea, and to hell with the body!" It seems to me that a lot of the ideas supposedly packed inside a jewel fall completely flat because the jewel has no relation to the body. Of what value is an idea when its medium of communication is a failure? Yes, dozens of times, I've myself tried to wear some of this super he-man, idea-packed jewelry. It's like being incarcerated in a straightjacket, and it's exactly at this point that the idea communication dies. If a designer really believes that the human body can be divorced from the jewel, then he's much better off trying to communicate his ideas through another medium — perhaps sculpture or painting.

It depresses me that handmade jewelry so often falls into a category labeled "useless objects of status." Do we bring this on ourselves? Or is it perhaps just another cancerous side effect of our industrialized mass culture? It's like a wall, and one wonders what it's really all about. You invest an idea within a piece of quality handwork, and then you and your work end up dumped into a label that paints you black as a "servant of snobs." And then you go home to reality — hardly any of us being able to make a living, being a kind of threatened minority in a nowhere land, ambiguously placed somewhere between art and handwork or art and industrial design. Our society invests everything it has in science and technology without concern for whether the investment is valid, and then it throws out a few scraps of leftover bread to the handworker.

Maybe we are partly to blame for our own condition. Maybe it has something to do with our failure to involve ourselves in the world at large. Maybe we isolate ourselves too much. Maybe it's our own fault that both our work and our profession are so often branded privileged. Is not the craftsman also an administrator of important values in our society?

Well, for one thing, I think we can take credit for generally upgrading the tastes of industry. We've provided a kind of stimulant or idea-drain for the stagnancy of industrial form. Perhaps we've also upgraded public tastes, and thereby forced industry to improve upon its own quality standards. But I'm not a negativist. I think hand craftsmanship is very much alive. The more industrialized we become, the greater the human need is for something original. Thus far, we've never managed without the original.

But if we hope to survive, then we've got to avoid compromise. We've got to give people the "whole" concept of quality. It's not enough to simply express an idea, or combine a lot of unusual materials. The expression has to be made as clearly as possible with as much honesty as possible and then realized with maximum skillfulness. If craftsmanship hopes to live alongside industry, then these conditions must be secured.

Sterling silver armband with beach-stone on leather.

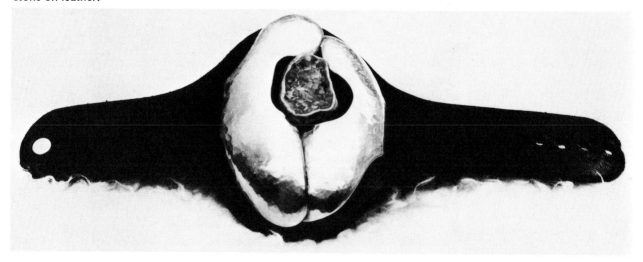

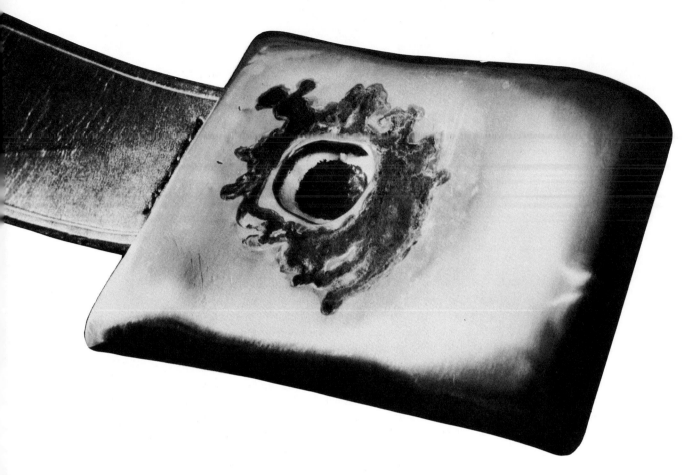

Fabricated brass belt buckle with
green enamel insert and oxidized
surfaces.

Fabricated brass belt buckle with
enamel insert and oxidized surfaces.

100

Necktie collar, front view. Formed silver with brass wire and leather.

Necktie collar, side view.

Matching armband and pendant in leather, rabbit fur, and macramé-knotted sisal. Strap is braided leather.

101

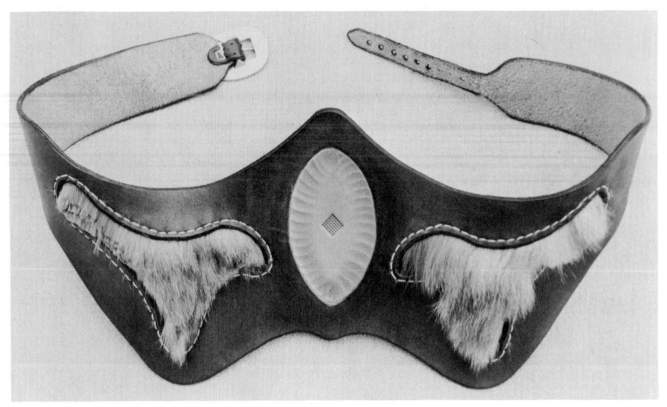

Belt in leather and fur. Buckle is
worn at the back.

"Stinker Status Choker." Necklace
choker is made from dyed plastic
garlic.

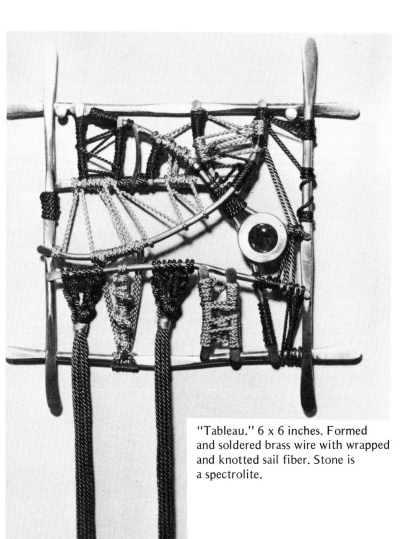

"Tableau." 6 x 6 inches. Formed
and soldered brass wire with wrapped
and knotted sail fiber. Stone is
a spectrolite.

Detail, macramé-knotted breast
form with glass beads.

Leather shoulder bag with
macramé-knotted flap.

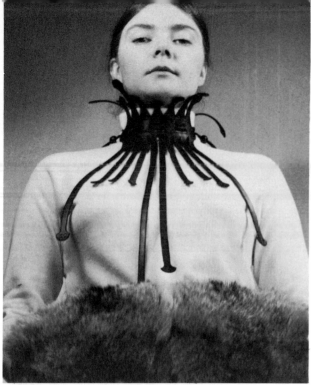

Leather collar with wooden beads,
side view.

Leather collar with wooden beads,
front view. Form is adjustable by a
closing mechanism at both sides.

Tar-yarn knotted body decoration
with fishing floats, front view.

104

Leather collar with wooden beads,
back view.

Body decoration with fishing floats,
back view.

105

Marcia Lewis
United States

Although she is an American, Marcia Lewis recently has been studying and working in Zurich, Switzerland.

For me to write an essay would be all the things an essay should not be. I'm too fresh out of graduate school, where an essay was a lot of crap to fill pages and satisfy unimaginative professors. No, I'd prefer to just talk to you about some thoughts I've had. So I'll just sit here by this beautiful window in my warm, cozy Zurich room, watch the snow gently fall, and pretend you're here too. Okay?

The making of ornaments for the body must truly be my chosen field. I've decided that anyone who can assemble someone else's designs for eight and one-half hours a day and still be excited and invigorated by working on one's own designs at night must be doing what God intended. To be using the same tools and techniques all day on repairing or constructing, while this hot new idea of your own is still on paper, is just killing. Then to have to quit your own work at midnight because money-work begins next morning at eight o'clock and your contact lenses feel like a couple of pieces of sandpaper on your eyes — well, it's all too frustrating. But finally that idea on paper somehow makes it into gold and feathers and a feeling of sheer jubilation explodes when I get to wear it to the party on Friday night. And an even more jubilant feeling comes when seeing how happy it can make someone else feel. Most jubilant feeling of all — the approval of other craftsmen. More rewarding than money in the bank. They know what effort, time, blood, and spirit it has in it — they appreciate that. It's like the 100 percent in red ink you used to get on your spelling papers in elementary school.

This great feeling can come in almost any material being worked with. It can be paint, clay, metal, fiber, chocolate-marshmallow frosting. It must come from the satisfaction of having the spark of an idea and the energy to carry it to completion. The craftsman has an advantage over a painter in that he is able to enjoy the work with more of his senses than merely his sight. He can touch it with his hand or foot or lips, smell it, and even taste it. And the one who can wear his creation is the luckiest of them all. I feel very sorry for men in a society which disapproves of them adorning themselves with ornaments. But I feel sorriest for men jewelers who never feel the excitement of wearing their own pieces. Did you know that not all good ornament makers (jewelers) are good businessmen? They come in different situations. One jeweler may own and operate a store, selling his work and living on his earnings. Another may sell his forms for only enough money to buy more materials and keep on working but be unable to live from his earnings. These are the two kinds of ornament makers I've found, anyway. The former finds a style or technique which sells, and then gradually cuts down on his creative process because it doesn't necessarily show a profit. The latter goes into some other business, which furnishes him with at least two-thirds of his income but doesn't keep him entirely away from his bench. Usually, but not always, these are our teachers. Rarely is there the combination of both. Usually one makes art, and one makes money.

For myself, at this time in my life, I am free to make what I like. My designs come to fit my needs. Going to Switzerland where it's cold? How about a leather and silver helmet with fur-lined ear flaps? Far out! Soon I may tire of it, but I made it, and I use it. When I do tire of it, it will probably be because of a new, more urgent idea to produce. That's the time when I'm a good person to know. The individual who happens to go for this piece will probably get to own it for the cost of my new idea. See? Just enough to keep me in materials so that all of my new ideas don't choke me to death.

But these are all thoughts coming from a student. I mean I was a student up until August, 1971, and too busy learning to compose any nice philosophies. It's crazy. Whenever I come to one conclusion that feels comfortable, I meet somebody with a different conclusion and it's reasonable — so goodbye to my first conclusion. Still, I'm constantly vacillating and changing; one piece rarely looks like another.

Don't know if I've said anything you can use, but if I go on it will just come out sounding like bullshit composition of every creative person I've ever admired. No good

Feather pin with hidden clasp.
18-carat gold and pheasant feathers.
Front silver plate is chased. The
tiny spouts that hold the feathers in
place were made in the same way
that one makes spouts for ceramic
teapots.

Feather pin, clasp detail.

Hat form. Carved in relief in pine
with woodcarving gouges.

A piece of leather was first soaked
and then nailed tight to the form
and into the relief pattern.

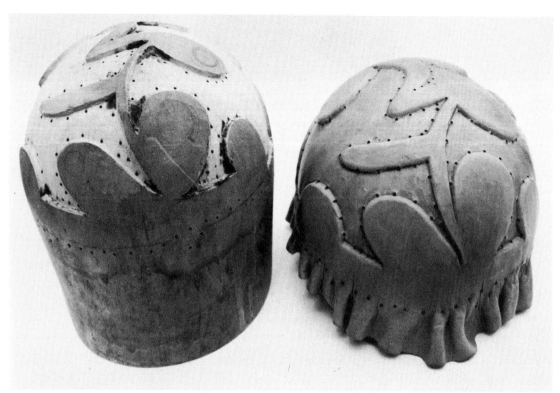

When dry, the leather was removed
from the form and then dyed.

Velvet-lined helmet in leather made
from the wood form. The helmet
includes lapin fur, East Indian
rosewood, silver, and moonstones.
The silver forms and moonstones
were riveted to the leather helmet
shell.

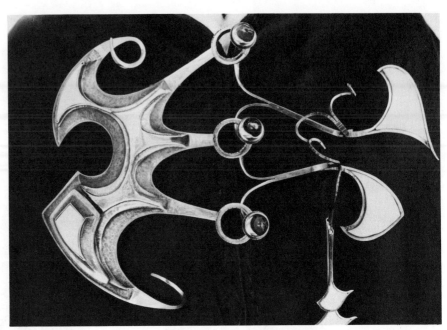

Clasp detail. The left side of the clasp also contains a concealed locket large enough to hold bus fare if the car conks out.

Cloak and clasp in glove leather with fur lining. Clasp is made from silver, ivory, smoky quartz.

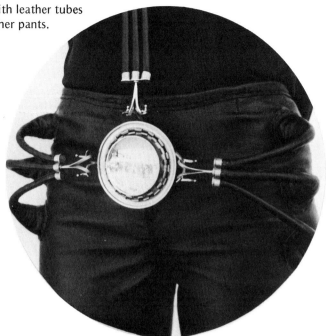

"Neck to Hip Ornament." Detail of center section with leather tubes sewn fast to leather pants.

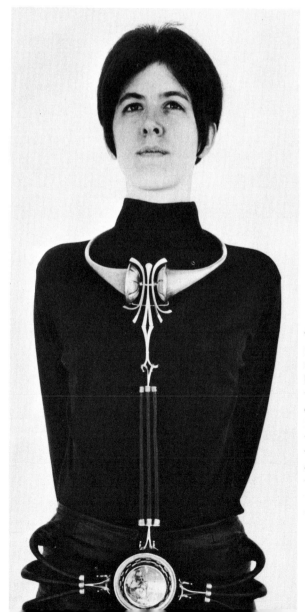

"Neck to Hip" ornament. The neckpiece consists of two horn-shaped forms in silver. These may be worn separately and apart from the rest of the construction. The center section of 3 slightly tapering leather tubes hooks into a silver form that holds a mirrored magnifying glass. From this point, the center form leads out to the hips via leather horn-shaped forms, which are finally sewn fast, directly onto the leather pants.

Winged armband in cast and fabricated sterling. The wings are
hinged to the center mask.

Winged armband, detail.

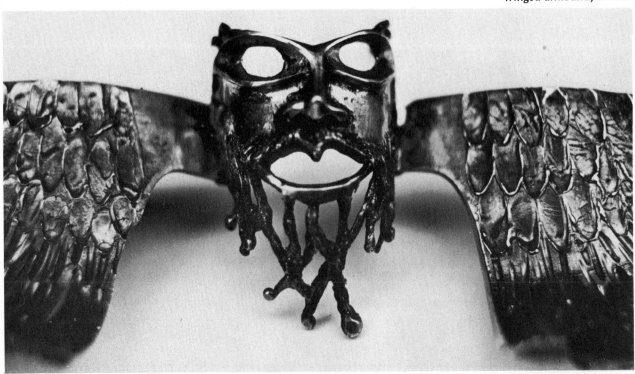

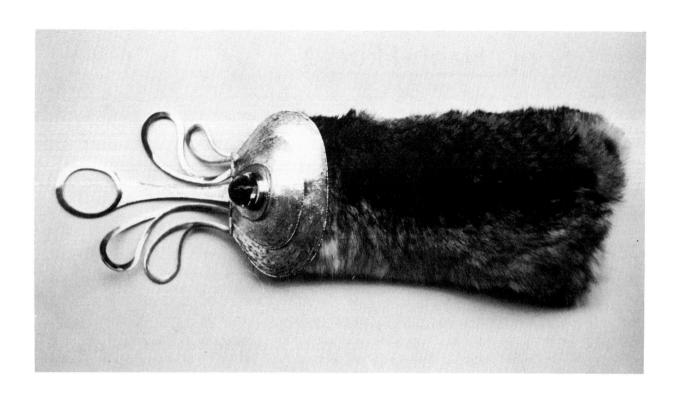

Chinchilla wrist muff in gray
chinchilla, sterling, and smoky
quartz.

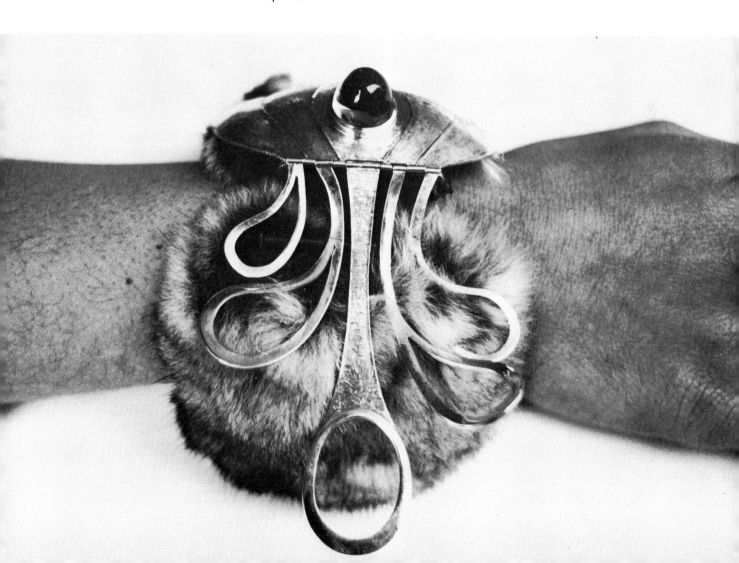

Sonja Hahn-Ekberg
Sweden

Sonja earns her living as a teacher in a music conservatory in Kalmar, Sweden. In the early part of the 1960s, she developed an interest in fibers and began expressing an explosive color personality in miniature embroidered icons — somewhat like tiny stained glass windows made of threads. These icons were designed to be hung on walls. Sonja decided she didn't care much for wall decorations, and so she began transforming her icons into jewelry — pendants, breast forms, armbands, and large brooches.

Sonja is a meticulous craftsman, often spending a week or even two weeks building a single form. She works in the evenings and on weekends after her music commitments are over. Her basic material is thread, mainly silk thread. Sometimes she does buy her thread, but usually, in order to get the colors or textures she wants, she picks up scraps of old material — even antique material — and then loosens or pulls each thread out from the woven material. In this way she reuses old thread within a new context. Whenever she can find it, she also uses gold and silver thread, and her forms very often contain tiny bits of fur, leather, and even seeds, glass beads, brass plates, or tiny brass nuts, washers, and bolts. Her work table is a collage of colors, scraps, and parts that she assembles into disciplined form.

Looking at her forms, one expects them to be fragile, but they are not. Although the eye experiences delicacy, the forms are rigidly constructed, durable, and functional.

Sonja normally begins a form from a rough sketch made in the actual size of the proposed piece. The basic parts or forms within the sketch are then transferred onto a heavy tagboard or poster quality paper. The pattern is then cut out and roughly proved to insure that the parts work together as planned. Sonja then begins a process of winding or wrapping single strands of thread around the tagboard pattern parts. She wraps tightly, avoiding overlap, and secures her thread ends on the back side with a sewing needle. The only complication in her technique is that it requires unbelievable patience, as well as finger skill. Her glass beads, seeds, nuts, and washers are sewn in place, and whenever fur or leather appear these materials are either sewn or glued in place. One can honestly say that Sonja works a bit in the same manner as a watchmaker — dealing with tiny parts and building her forms bit by bit.

Thread jewelry from fabric scraps, glue, cardboard, scissors, and a sewing needle? Can this be jewelry? Well, at least Scandinavians obviously think so. Sonja's work has been supported with unbelievable enthusiasm, and only on very rare occasions does she return from an exhibition with unsold forms. If there is such a thing as modern jewelry that is the antithesis of the industrial age, Sonja's forms are about as close as one can come. She says this:

> Me? Who am I? I work with music and textiles simply
> because it is my way to live — and, hopefully, survive. To
> accomplish something with my hands is for me somewhat like
> experiencing a wild strawberry field. It's also a nice feeling
> inside when I feel useful and when I stand the chance of making
> somebody else happy.

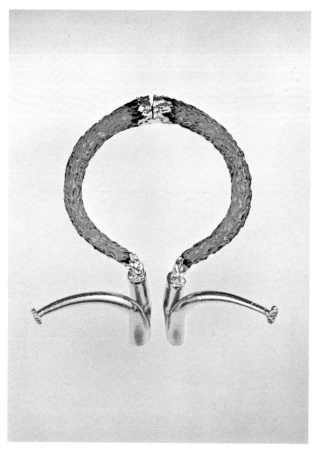

Torque of green polyester and
electroformed silver gilt. *Stanley
Lechtzin.*

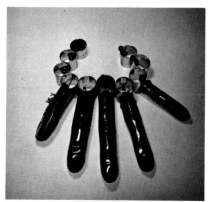

Necklace in silver with several
stones and pearls. *Barbara Gasch.*

Silver, leather, and feather bracelet.
Arline Fisch.

Crocheted shoulder bag. *Mary Lou
Higgins.* Lynx fur, beads, feathers,
and acrilon fiber.

"The Rough Ones." *Edward
Koelling.* Pendant cast in silver with
fur trim.

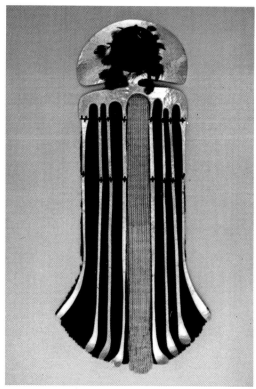

Brooch. *Richard Mafong and Jon Riis*. Strip weaving, using gold plate, pheasant feathers, and gold beads.

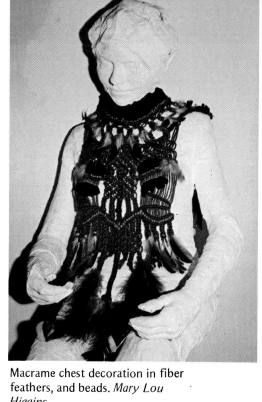

Macrame chest decoration in fiber feathers, and beads. *Mary Lou Higgins.*

Macramé-knotted body decoration in fishing fiber with glass beads. *Marita Kulvik.*

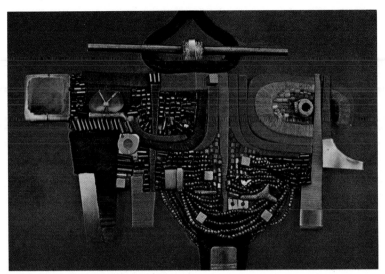

Breast pendant from glass beads,
silk threads, pieces of leather, and
glass washers. *Sonja Hahn-Ekberg.*

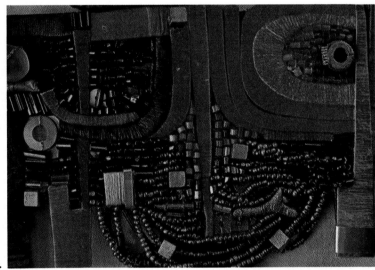

Breast pendant, detail.

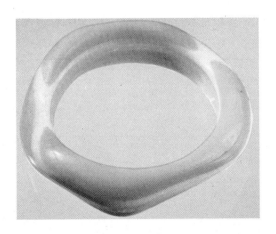

Laminated acryl armband. *Olli
Tamminen.*

Industrialism is a vast word. Although it is necessary, it seems to swallow everything. And despite its vastness, industry does need hand craftsmen and artists.

So with full sails forward, one must dare to do something. So I try.

Armband. Made from silk threads, leather, and brass washers. Armband core is tagboard wrapped with thread.

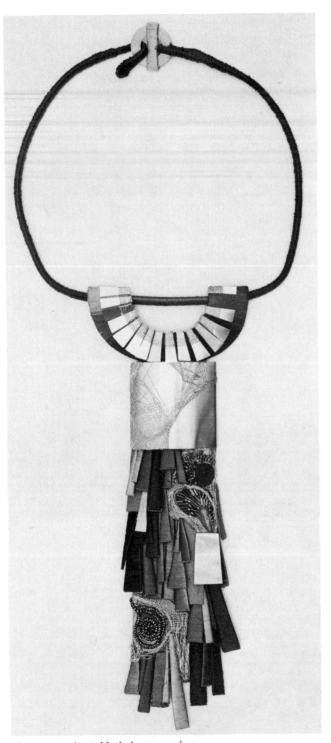

Breast pendant. Made by wrapping threads over tagboard and then sewing and gluing the assemblage in place.

Breast pendant with silk threads, brass washers, and glass beads. Wrapped, sewn, and glued.

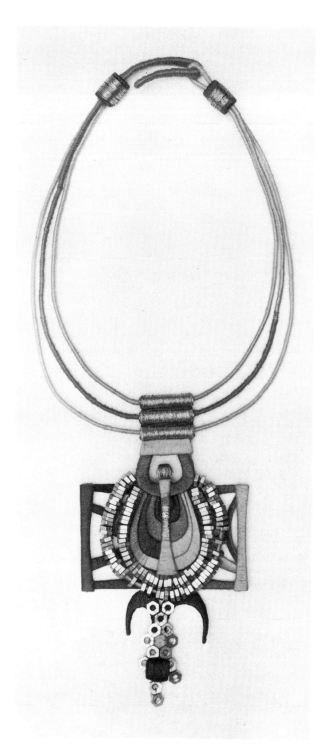

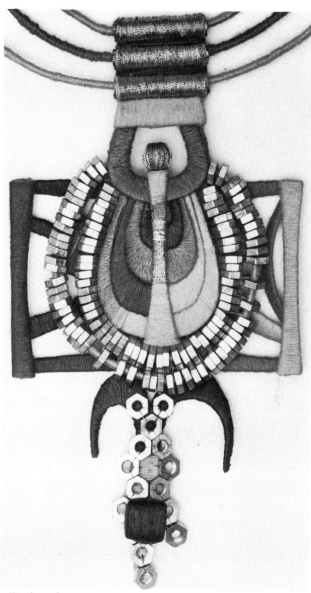

Breast pendant with silk threads,
brass washers, and brass nuts.
Wrapped, sewn, and glued.

Brooch. Made from silk threads,
glass beads, brass washers, and
seeds. Wrapped, sewn, and glued.

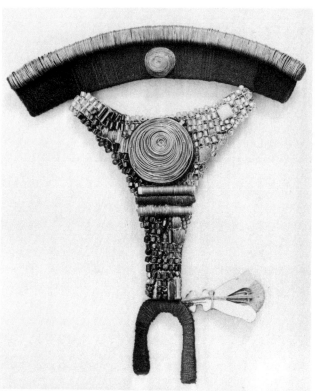

Brooch. Made from silk threads,
glass beads, pieces of brass, and
coiled brass wire. Wrapped, sewn,
and glued.

Brooch. Made from appliquéd
leather, silk threads, glass beads,
seeds, and pieces of brass. Wrapped,
sewn, and glued.

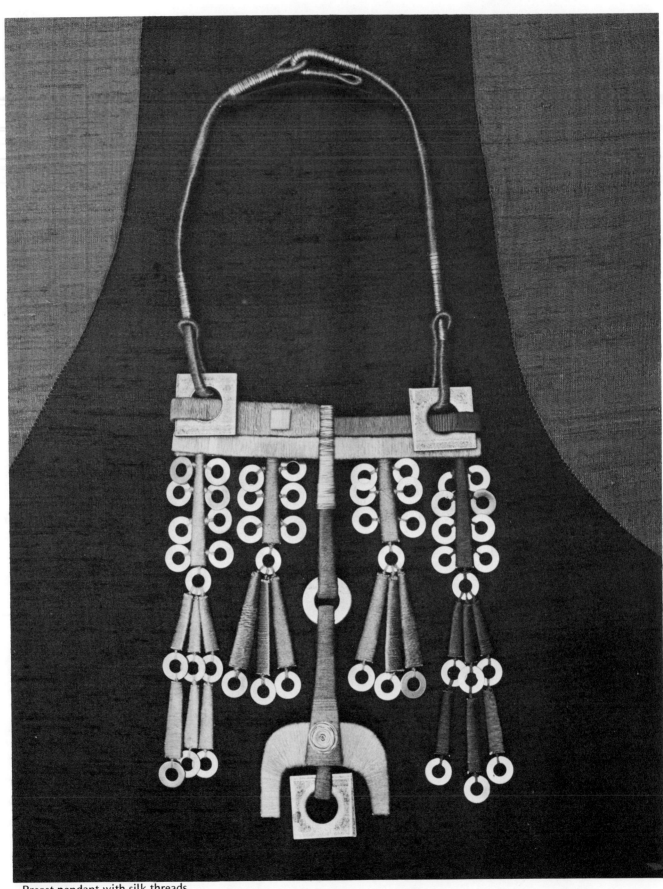

Breast pendant with silk threads,
brass washers, and coiled brass wire.
Wrapped, sewn, and glued.

Sonja sorts out thread at her work-
table. Most of her threads are
pulled loose from previously woven
fabrics.

Sonja's construction technique
involves tightly wrapped threads
around a core of tagboard.

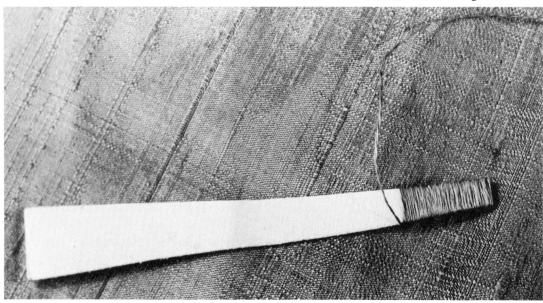

Clifton Nicholson, Jr.
United States

Cliff kept writing letters, with every intention of contributing something in words about his work. But instead of writing something himself he contributed only a magazine article (missing its first page) wherein a now anonymous journalist wrote words about Cliff. The article had been sandwiched into the magazine next to a full-page advertisement for Oscar Ewing's Returnable Milk Cartons.

The article Cliff sent is a total journalistic disaster, but it at least serves as an example of the irresponsible coverage very often given to creative people by the press. Needless to say, the journalist in question might just as well have been writing about returnable milk cartons for all the insight he expressed about Cliff's work. Among other useless items (which say not one word about Cliff's work), the reporter tells us that "when Cliff was a small boy back home in Indiana, he used to collect chicken feathers." One wonders what Freud would have predicted for an Indiana Hoosier who collected chicken feathers.

Yes, Cliff works with feathers, but he also works with metal and many other materials as well. As you see from his form contributions, Cliff has progressed a very long way since those slim chicken feather days in Indiana. A more expressive fantasy than his would be difficult to find anywhere.

One additional footnote on this hopeless magazine article Cliff sent — the reporter, upon realizing that Cliff made jewelry out of feathers, apparently became concerned that if Cliff were to decide to mass-produce his feathered forms, it might prove disastrous "to the existence of animals." Isn't it just like the press not to know that feathers don't too often grow on animals? But then, at least when the question of animal extinction was posed, Cliff was gentle enough to assure the reporter that he had "nothing at all against animals." Perhaps, after all, that article really did have something to do with Oscar Ewing's Returnable Milk Cartons?

Feather collar with feather and cast yellow gold rings.

This ring is made
from the beak and crest of the
silver pheasant. The ring shank is
from cast yellow gold.

Peacock cape and headdress.

Headdress, detail.

Collar. Made from crocheted wool
backing with appliquéd peacock
breast feathers.

126

Ring. Made from the beak and crest
of a Lady Amherst pheasant. The
ring shank was cast in green gold
with added sterling silver lines
inside the mouth.

Two rings. Left, ring shank cast in yellow gold. Includes a shark's tooth and the natural red feathers from the crest of a Lady Amherst pheasant. Right, ring shank cast in yellow gold. Includes a shark's tooth and the natural orange feathers from a cock-of-the-rock.

128

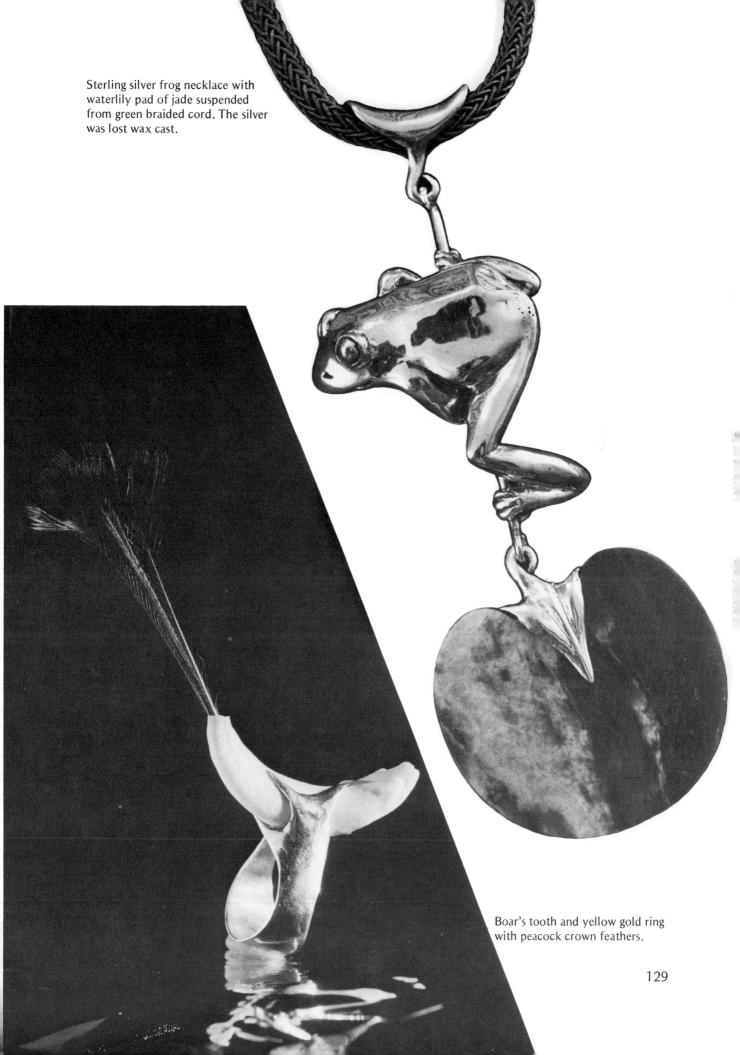

Sterling silver frog necklace with
waterlily pad of jade suspended
from green braided cord. The silver
was lost wax cast.

Boar's tooth and yellow gold ring
with peacock crown feathers.

129

Loughborough College of Art and Design

England

Keith Smith, the jewelry leader at the Loughborough College of Art and Design in Leicestershire, managed to arrange a school jewelry project in cooperation with the British Steel Corporation. The project involved designing body forms using stainless steel. Many of Keith's students became seriously involved in the project, and later, after the project had been completed, Keith invited two of the participants, Frank Taylor and Douglas Wagstaffe, to comment upon their involvement.

Frank Taylor

Three years ago, during my second year at art college, it occurred to me that there were two basic things wrong with jewelry: (1) the areas of the body generally regarded as being able to accept jewelry were few and unnecessarily limited, and (2) the nature of most of the jewelry produced was strongly biased toward sweetness and preciousness. I also disagreed with the view that an item of jewelry could be universally good or universally bad. I believe that pieces of jewelry are tools of psychology, their job being to make the wearer look more attractive, but more important even than this, to make the wearer *feel* more attractive and therefore be in a better state of mind. A morale booster indeed. Anything which does this — from the cheapest plastic bead to the most enormous diamond — is, in my opinion, jewelry.

The first problem I encountered in trying to change other people's minds about the nature of jewelry was to practice what I preached. In order to do this, I listed all the main areas normally used for the display of jewelry — fingers, wrist, neck, arms, ears, and toes. I immediately determined not to use any of these areas in my own work. To continue, I made another list including those areas which were not normally included for display of jewelry — the nose, nostrils, shoulders, forehead, knees, buttocks, crotch, and mouth. In order to be consistent with my explorations, I determined that these were the very areas in which I should concentrate my forms.

I made two additional lists: one listed all of the "precious" materials normally used in jewelry, and the other listed all the inexpensive, common yet attractive materials which could be used. The only other preparation left was to think up ways of making jewelry less sweet, more repulsive, but yet doing so in a more or less intriguing manner. I made another list, this time of repulsive images — skin infections, insects, frogs, snakes, grubs, indeed anything likely to produce the desired effect.

I was fortunate, at this point in my training, to be given the opportunity to put my ideas into practice. I was asked, along with others in the department, to take part in a project promoting stainless steel for the British Steel Corporation. The only condition of the project brief was that stainless steel should be used in a new, exciting way that would "astound the public"!

After several uninspired attempts at some sort of "exciting" piece of decoration, I produced a steel face mask. The piece was basically a piece of curved sheet, which fitted over the ears and onto which were fitted stainless steel eyelashes. The eyelashes were mounted on short springs so that they quivered when the head was moved. The lower edge of the mask was shaped in a series of "roaming tentacles" which intruded into the cheeks and mouth. The thing looked, felt, and indeed was, very uncomfortable. I did, however, what I had set out to do. I avoided the conventional areas. I avoided the conventional treatment, and I concentrated on impact, rather than practicality. This piece set me off on the type of work I am now interested in. There followed a series of masquerade masks in cheap, bright card, combining unusual decoration and cheap materials; then came a period of gimmicky items — string vests, macramé and beech chokers, rubber knee pads, even a "primitive" chest decoration made from motorcycle parts and string! These pieces were really exercises to get me working in a way different from the norm, and they proved very useful. However, they lacked one important ingredient. I had for a long time been convinced that repulsive images are very often attractive — hence the success of such experiences as horror films. I found, however, that the repulsive quality was better if it was simulated rather than actual. The recipient must always have the reassurance that it is not real. It seems that people are often eager to be both frightened and repulsed if they understand that the whole experience is only pretense.

The first finished piece to come out of this investigation was a head ornament. If women wear wigs as a way of immediately changing their appearance, then why shouldn't they wear decorated wigs? During the British Steel Corporation project, I had done several experiments with various sections of stainless steel, and I found the material perfect for what I was trying to do. Stainless steel was very strong in thin wire form, it had a shine, and it was flexible enough to move at the slightest touch. I made many lengths of stainless coil, using very thin wire and then twisting these coils to give the impression of writhing worms. The coils were very strong. I sewed them onto a manufactured wig. They had a shine which was suggestive of smooth, wet skin, and they wiggled at every movement of the head. The effect was that of a repulsive Medusa; but the piece had the practical ease of a head ornament.

From this point, I sort of fell into a period of stagnation during which I made some small items — things like stick-on silver warts, repulsive nose-clips, and phallic pendants using tapered steel springs. But nothing produced the effect I was aiming for. Eventually however, I developed an idea for a G-string. I had been working on a chastity belt idea, but I wanted to combine the "armor" aspect with the satirical or funny side as well. The term G-string has many connotations. None of them are particularly negative; most are amusing, fascinating, even a bit sensual. The G-string I eventually made is a shaped piece of stainless steel on which are fastened some 200 tapered stainless steel springs of varying lengths, all twisted in different directions like a handful of writhing snakes. It is fastened to the crotch by three chains — two around the waist and one under the crotch — all three meeting and fastening around the back of the waist. The springs proved ideal for suggesting a pubic hair, serpent image. And the whole piece, with its chains and sheet back plate giving ample reference to armor, is padded and backed with lipstick-red leather. I did this deliberately to give some indication of the qualities of intrigue, repulsion, tartness, and excitement which I think jewelry should have at this particular point in time.

Strangely enough, or maybe not so strangely, it took me two weeks to find a model willing to pose for photographs wearing the piece!

Stainless steel G-string. *Frank Taylor.*

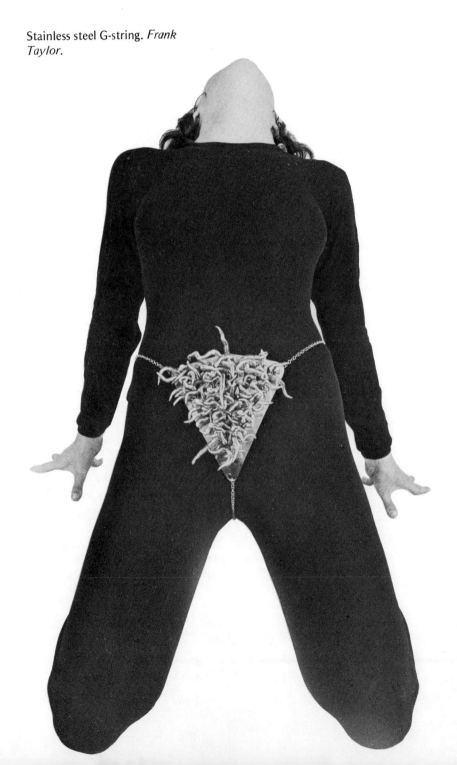

Stainless steel mask. *Frank Taylor*.

Douglas Wagstaffe

At the time the steel jewelry was made, a list of techniques for treating the material was comprised. I had never before worked in stainless steel so it was to be a new experience. It had various limitations, but I tried to carry through with the forms I had been exploring in ferrous metals. Success proved to be only a matter of experimentation, or putting the steel through various metal techniques in order to achieve my forms.

The idea behind the project was for promotional purposes to create new markets for steel. In other words, to explore the idea that steel could be both versatile and beautiful.

The yolk collar or breastplate I made was formed from steel sheet and then beaten, planished, drilled, and oxidized to a gold color. I wanted a large expanse of reflective surface. The collar may suggest a piece of armor, but I can only define it as an "extravagant body adornment." I also made a chain mail neck decoration with earrings. This was probably more applicable to wear, as the form proportions were more reasonable. The chain mail was based on traditional chain mail design and constructed from separate steel links. The bottom part was pierced with a welding torch to make a craterlike surface.

Another piece I made was a torch-pierced collar. This was constructed from separate fins of pierced steel. The torch achieved a craterlike effect, which I combined with a polished surface. I think the whole thing resulted in a powerful decorative surface.

These are only my own ways of working the stainless. Other students found all manner of ways. I found the material exciting to use and capable of producing many effects. I have no complicated reason as to why the forms came about. They were just born out of many interesting experiments. The whole thing was of course made possible through the help of the staff and equipment at Loughborough.

Hammered and drilled stainless steel collar. Earrings cut with a welding torch. *Douglas Wagstaffe.*

134

Hammered and burned collar in
stainless steel. *Douglas Wagstaffe.*
Head ornament in stainless,
Georgina Thomas.

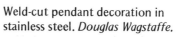

Weld-cut pendant decoration in
stainless steel. *Douglas Wagstaffe.*

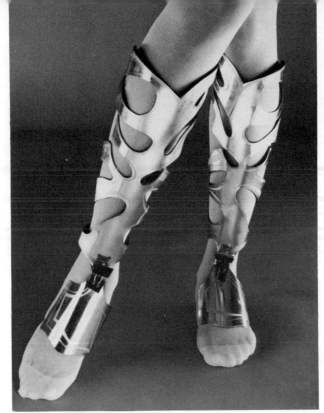

Etched stainless steel leggings.
Elizabeth Coslett.

Stainless steel necklace made from
hammered stainless wire. *Lesley
Barlow.*

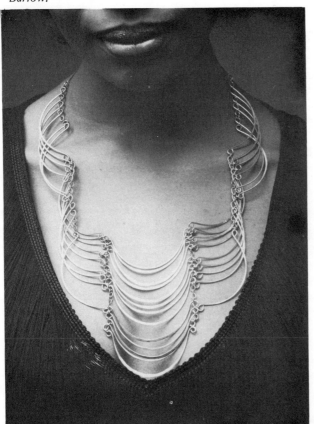

Earrings and necklace in stainless
steel wire. *Denyse Little.*

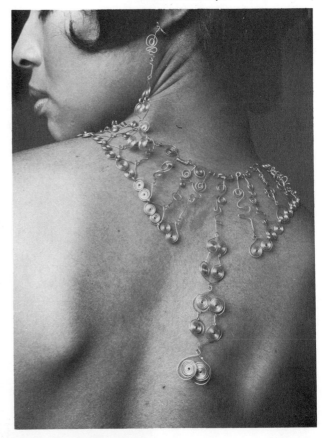

Stainless steel necklace and earrings. *Kate Walker.*

Neckband in stainless steel from straw-braiding technique. *John Baldwin.* Headpiece in stainless knitted wire. *Georgina Thomas.*

Ann Marie Shillito
England

Jewelry should be worn as clothing is worn — to enhance the personality and to express mood. It should be worn every day and not just for special occasions.

I do not use precious metals very often. I concentrate mainly on steel and titanium, and I design for mass production and for forms of limited edition. My work in mass production necessitates a knowledge of tool-making and production methods and a willingness to accept the interaction and cooperation from others involved who have differing priorities. Tight limitations are imposed, and these are very stimulating, even if somewhat frustrating. I therefore enjoy the balance I have of designing both experimental pieces and limited editions — where I can impose my own limitations. Apart from steel and titanium being inexpensive, which allows their use in greater volume, titanium can be anodized by heat and electrolysis into a greater range of beautiful colors.

I feel I work better when I am limited by the properties of the metal I'm using. Perhaps the reason is that the many small decisions that have to be made when the field is wide open are nonexistent, and I can therefore concentrate on more important, larger decisions. When I design a buckle or a necklace, for example, I begin with the fastening. I try to integrate this into the decoration or have it grow into part of the main feature. Function is very often where the idea for the design begins its spiral.

Over a period of two years, I designed and made a body adornment in steel. This project was purely academic, and the restrictions for this type of jewelry had to be realized. It had to be custom made. The opportunities to wear it were limited, and the form had to be inexpensive. It was quite a challenge to design around the whole body comfortably. This is why it took so long to realize the steel form. It had to be redesigned and modified, and a linking system had to evolve which could make it comfortable to wear.

Another challenge for me is to determine a new, different place to wear jewelry. I designed two pieces to wear over the hip: one a brooch with hanging perspex domes that move and sway when walking and the other a buckle with the main part over the hip, again with hanging pieces — silver spheres and wires as the decoration and delicate contrast against the titanium.

I expect I will go on working in titanium and steel for a good while yet. It's the same with most materials — the longer you work with them, the more infinite their possibilities become.

Titanium and perspex hip ornament. The titanium has been
electrolitically oxidized to a pink
color. The form has two hooks
adhered to the back to fasten to
clothing. Two perspex domes were
sandwiched onto a titanium
component to form the droplet, all
of which were pierced out on a
pantograph.

Titanium necklace with titanium
buckle prototype. The necklace
center piece is oxidized blue and
has been "sprung" onto the neckband as the fastening mechanism.
The three pieces hanging from the
necklace are removable. The buckle
is saw-pierced out with the center
back area anodized blue by
electrolosis.

Stainless steel buckles and chain
belts for mass production. Buckle
designed so that one component
reversed interlocks with another to
form the buckle. The chain belts
can be shortened to form either a
necklace or a bracelet.

Antti Siltavouri
Finland

Antti Siltavouri is an industrial designer. He spends his professional life helping in the design of trucks for the Sisu Manufacturing Company of Finland. His work at Sisu brings him into almost daily contact with fiberglass and acryl — the firm uses both of these materials in the construction of prototypes and truck cabs. From trucks to jewelry was not necessarily a logical route; nevertheless Antti went the route because of his interest in the potentials of acryl.

Acryl is available in sheet, block, chunk, and powder form. It is available completely colorless (transparent) or it can be obtained in a whole spectrum of ready-made impregnated colors. Form building with acryl can be done by heating and bending, by reducing or grinding, by casting, or by combining these techniques within the same piece.

Antti uses perhaps the least complicated approach in building acryl form — heating and bending a flat surface into three-dimensional form. He works with sheet acryl, usually varying in thickness from three to five millimeters. The acryl he uses is called ICI. It is manufactured by Imperial Chemical Industries Limited, England. This same firm also manufactures a special cement or bonding agent that is used to bond together pieces of ICI. The cement is called Tensol Cement Number 6. It is a one-component, transparent cement that begins to harden in about ten minutes and is completely hard-bonded after about thirty minutes. Similar sheet acryl and bonding agents are available all over the world. Antti uses ICI only because it happens to be readily available in Finland.

On some of his forms Antti uses only one piece of acryl, but on other forms he may combine as many as two or three pieces. Regardless of how many pieces of acryl he may use, he always begins his form-building by first working the forms out on paper or thin tagboard. Once he's decided upon a form, he cuts out a paper pattern for each piece involved and then explores the bending possibilities, bending the flat paper pieces into dimensional form and exploring the juxtaposition of forms within the form. After he knows where he's going with bending, he makes a duplicate pattern for each form piece, glues these pattern pieces directly onto the acryl sheet, and cuts the forms out from the acryl using a standard jeweler's saw with a medium-fine blade.

To bend the sheet acryl, Antti uses nothing more than his kitchen oven, set at about 180 degrees centigrade (382 degrees F.) and a pair of leather work gloves. The form pieces are placed in the oven for five to eight minutes, or until the acryl becomes easily pliable. Gloves are worn to prevent burning the fingers while bending. Care should be taken not to overheat acryl. There have been many cases where amateur craftsmen have placed acryl in either an enamel or ceramic kiln, only to find that a few minutes later it explodes. And if the acryl piece is large enough it is possible to blow the door right off of a small enamel kiln.

After his acryl is pliable, Antti does his bending quickly in order to keep the form lines as spontaneous as possible. He of course knows exactly where

142

he's going because he has practiced his bending first on the paper pattern. If he should make a mistake in bending, the acryl can be reheated and re-formed. If the final form involves more than one piece of acryl, he usually bends the pieces together, holding them at their junction point, as for example, the junction point of the band on a finger ring. In this way (holding and bending the pieces together), the pieces will fit or flow to form when later cemented. Once the pieces are all bent properly, the acryl is allowed to cool at room temperature.

Antti's next step in construction is to cement form pieces together with acryl cement, apply a clamp to the bonded area, and then allow the cement to dry. If a finger ring is involved, he reams out the finger hole with a reaming bit attached to an electric drill. From this point on, he refines form surfaces and form edges by using files, sandpaper, emery paper, and, finally, by using a polishing cloth.

Armband. One piece of twisted and polished acryl.

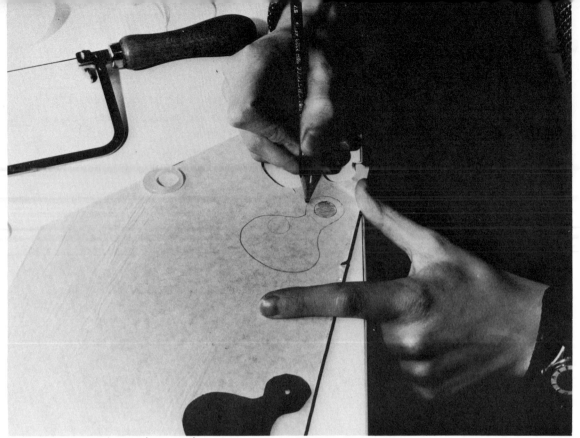

Ring form is traced onto sheet acryl from a paper pattern.

Form is cut from sheet using a jeweler's saw with a medium-fine blade.

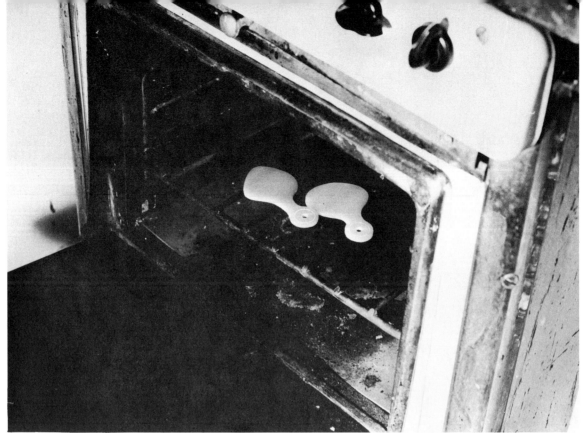

Form pieces are placed in a kitchen oven set at 180° C. (382° F.) and left for 5 to 8 minutes, or until pliable.

Wearing gloves, Antti bends the pliable acryl pieces together while holding them tightly at the ring band junction.

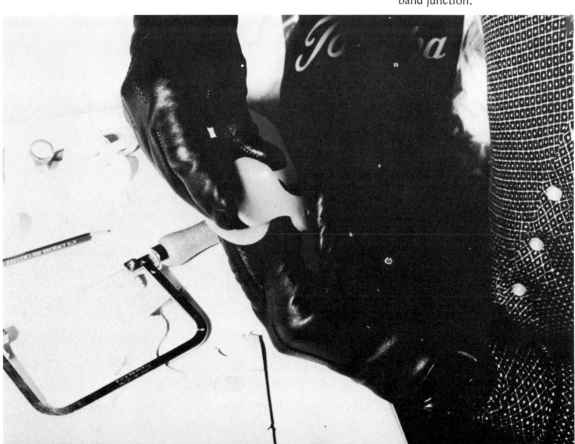

After pieces are bent to form, they
are laminated with acryl cement.

The cemented pieces are clamped
together until dry.

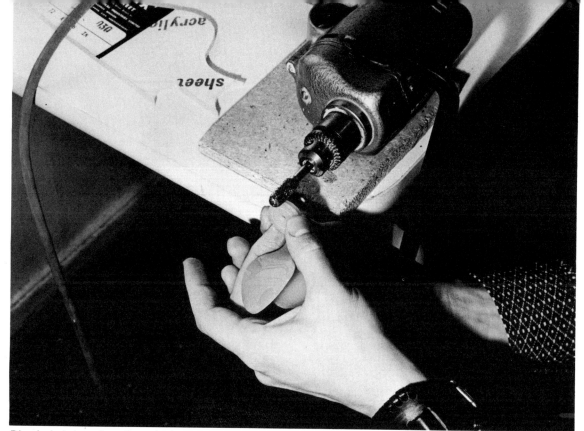

Ring hole is bored, and acryl edges
are polished with an electric drill,
using a reaming bit.

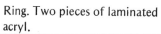

Ring. Two pieces of laminated
acryl.

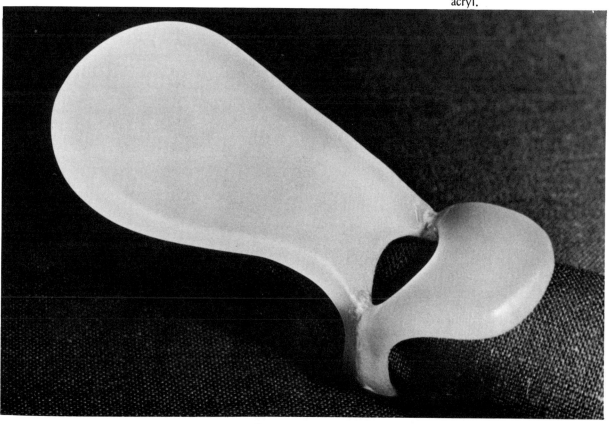

Ring. Two pieces of transparent,
wine-colored laminated acryl. Edges
are still unfinished.

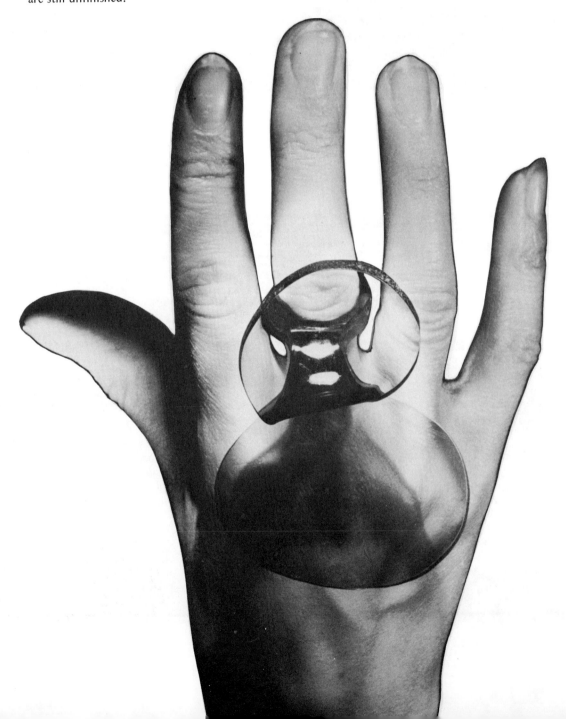

Ring. Two pieces of transparent,
laminated acryl. Edges are still
unfinished.

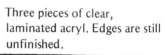

Three pieces of clear,
laminated acryl. Edges are still
unfinished.

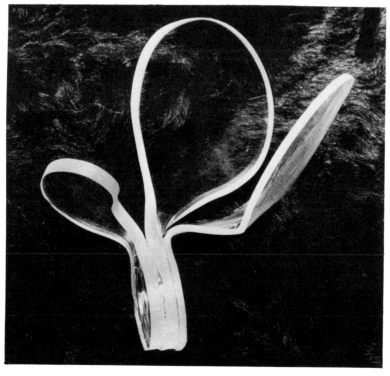

Olli Tamminen
Finland

Olli has been into using acryl for jewelry since the early 1960s. In 1963, when Finland sent a few of his forms to the Milan Triennale, Olli's rings were in fact so well received that most of them were stolen by spectators!

Olli builds his acryl forms in quite another way than Antti Siltavouri. Olli's technique involves laminating layers of acryl together into a solid, and then reducing the solid to a final jewel form. In order to cut down on the amount of reducing, he saws out his pieces as close to the final form as possible. To laminate his layers, he also uses transparent acryl cement.

As he builds his solid from layers, Olli very often graduates or even contrasts his acryl colors with several colors or tones of color appearing in the same piece. To reduce the laminated block to final form, Olli uses electric grindstones, reaming bits, and files. On most of his forms, he polishes surfaces smooth and scratch-free with an electric polishing wheel, rouge, and a cloth buffer. Polishing must be done a little at a time, and gently, so as not to cause excess friction or overheating in the acryl.

Olli's forms are mostly organic and three dimensional — they have no reverse side. In addition to using acryl, he has also realized many of his forms in reindeer horn, leather, and fur.

Laminated acryl ring.

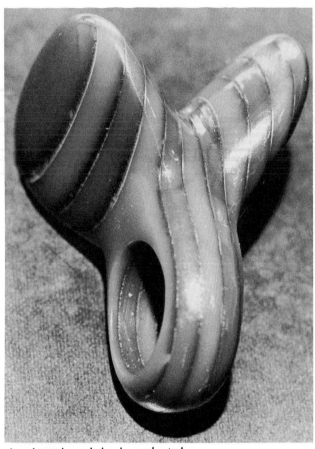

Laminated acryl ring in graduated
color tones. Side view.

Laminated acryl ring, front view.

Leather and fur ring.

Laminated acryl ring.

Loose "sandwich" acryl ring. The
layers of this ring are stacked
loosely so that they can be moved
or rotated to change the
composition.

154

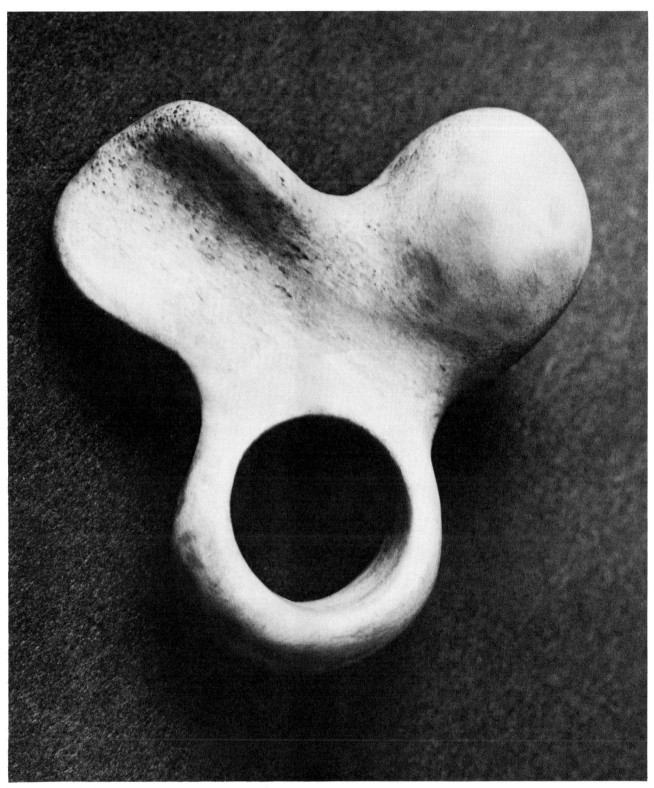

Ring in carved reindeer horn.

Gunilla Treen

England

I enjoy combining several different materials — perspex, silver, gold, ivory, titanium, resin, in fact anything which I find reflects the mood of the other materials used. My pieces are rarely designed before they are made. They are assembled, often from pieces lying around me. The forms grow as they are made. Therefore, I am free to take a variety of different directions during form construction, and it is often difficult to decide which way to go. Through this method, I find I have a surplus of ideas. This has led me to a speed of working which is suited to the type of work I do. Each of my pieces is therefore made as a simple statement and rarely repeated.

My pieces are not a gallery for displaying technical skill. I require only that the piece look clean and sharp. I often wish I were more mechanically minded, but then again, the simple mechanics come to me naturally.

"Cloudscape" brooch in perspex and titanium. Gunilla was trying to "capture a feeling from a children's pop-up picture book" in this piece. She was trying to "gain both a brooch and an object-picture." The titanium has been anodized.

156

"Rain" brooch in perspex,
titanium, resin, ivory, and silver.

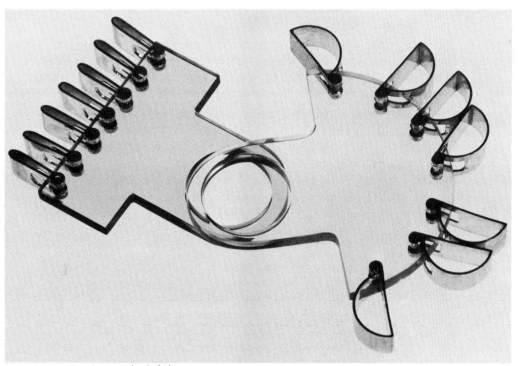

Two rings. The ring on the left is
made from transparent green
perspex with movable silver flaps.
The ring on the right is made from
pink perspex.

Bjorn Weckstrom
Finland

Bjorn Weckstrom began as a goldsmith. Without any doubt, he is today the man most responsible for injecting life back into Europe's industrial production of jewelry. His working partnership with Kruunu Koru of Finland is the next best thing to a jewelry craftsman's utopia.

To sum up the whole experience, it is enough to say that, despite overwhelming odds, Bjorn and Kruunu Koru grew . . . and grew . . . and grew — just like the beanstalk that Jack planted. And the experience is a revelation that the energy we call "creativity" is a kind of perpetual motion. You give a man one plus, and he returns two. You give him two, and he returns four, and so forth, until you have more positive results than anyone had anticipated. And in the final analysis, both the giver and the receiver have redefined everything.

I own a piece of jewelry that Bjorn handmade back in the very early part of the 1960s. That piece contains only a tiny seed of the form-giving Bjorn Weckstrom potentials of the 1970s. Bjorn, too, has grown . . . and grown . . . and grown. His seed was watered, and it burst forth with fruit. I doubt that the Bjorn of the early 1960s was even himself aware of what was creatively inside him. It required the watering and the sunshine to bring it out. This is true of all of us. Perhaps even better than half of our creativity lies undiscovered, unused, and frustrated within us. We all need watering, and we all need our share of creative sunshine.

The really beautiful footnote to Bjorn's experience with Kruunu Koru is the total absence of negativism. The mentality of the creative craftsman and the mentality of business industry can get along. Bjorn is living proof. Complaints? If he has any, they are not directed toward Kruunu Koru. Has he sold his private soul to the devil industry? Has he made himself a cog in an enormous industrial jewelry machine? Has he confused a few scraps of bread and a slice of ego for happily-ever-afterland? Well, for those doubting Thomases who have experienced battle scars at the hands of industry, the answer in Bjorn's case is an emphatic no! Bjorn has been neither abused nor exploited. I have known and observed Bjorn for the past six years. His industrial relationship really works!

In the beginning of the 1970s, just after Bjorn had successfully launched his "Space-Silver" series of human figures immersed in seas of silver, he began exploring the potentials for combining silver and acryl within the same piece. Bjorn describes the experience this way.

Why do I combine silver and acryl? Actually, I'm not that sure. Perhaps I wanted to include and involve a space around my forms — in other words, connect space to the form. I think the translucent acryl creates a bridge between the space and the silver. Perhaps there are other reasons. Perhaps I like to see the silver landscape of the form continue — continue into a bubbling, translucent, weightless environment. Why do I combine silver with acryl? Well, somebody has to tell me.

Bjorn worked out his first silver-acryl prototypes in polyester. He hand-cast these forms in silicone rubber molds. They were rough, the material was milky, and the prototypes were without excitement for either the eye or the touch. Having tried polyester prototypes, he then turned to building wax and plaster models. This procedure produced favorable results. The polyester method was therefore abandoned. From this rough beginning, Bjorn and Kruunu Koru were able to discover acryl, to control it, and to produce in a series a sophisticated blending of two totally different materials. Needless to say, the experience was not without its technical problems.

Unlike the previous examples of acryl form illustrated in this book, Bjorn's acryl forms are cast, from an acryl powder in about the consistency of sugar. The acryl forms are cast within hand-carved, hard steel molds (not stainless steel). Each mold is carved in two halves. The two mold halves fit within an acryl induction casting machine — an enormous, belching machine whose cost would wipe out the life savings of about twenty goldsmiths.

Acryl powder is poured into a "hopper" on the machine. This powder is heated to about 300 degrees centigrade. The resulting liquid then flows, by a combination of gravity and pressure, through a tube and into an opening in one-half of the steel mold. While this goes on, the two mold halves are being pressed together under tension. As the liquid acryl flows into the space of the mold, the air that was in the mold is trapped and absorbed into the acryl in the form of abstract bubbles. Meanwhile, a jet of cold water is directed on the mold, and this immediately cools the acryl. The mold opens automatically, and out drops an acryl form. It is completely transparent, and within it are trapped bubbles of air — the bubbles are never exactly alike. Bjorn makes use of these random air bubbles, but if one doesn't want them within the acryl an escape route must be provided for the air in the mold — something like an air-exhaust tube — so the air can be either forced or sucked out of the mold as the acryl is induced into the mold. Kruunu Koru has also learned that the induction machine must always be kept clean. This eliminates the possibility of foreign matter appearing within the acryl.

On many of his forms, Bjorn has given the acryl a taste of color, but not a solid color. Bjorn does not approve of placing a color base right within the casting acryl. He feels that the standard colors made for this purpose are dull, undefined, and in conflict with silver. He feels that when one colors a whole piece of acryl the chance for color spontaneity is lost. The same is true for color subtlety. What you end up with in solid color acryl is a loss of transparency, and a "frosted," opaque feeling that makes the material look almost sick in the worst sense of being plastic.

Instead of using solid acryl colors, Bjorn injects color into the acryl form after it is cast. He's tried many types of colors, including dry powder colors, special acryl colors, and even water-base colors. After the acryl form is cast, a tiny hole is drilled into one or more of the bubbles. A drop or two of color is injected, and then the drill hole is sealed shut by filling it with a sliver of acryl cemented in place with acryl cement. If Bjorn wants to suspend liquid color within the acryl permanently, he uses the same procedure, except that he mixes the color with alcohol.

The trickiest part on the acryl form is the finishing, particularly the polishing. Acryl is an aggressive heat conductor, and therefore tends to crack if it is cooled too fast. If hard polishing is required, the acryl must be allowed to cool slowly in warm water, allowing the water to cool off by itself together with the acryl. Another point in polishing is to try and maintain an even heat all the way through the whole acryl form. If the polishing becomes too hard and too violent, the "skin" of the acryl heats up ahead of the "body," and cracking, or "checking," may result. Gentleness is the answer.

Once the acryl form is finished, it is cemented to the silver form under pressure. These silver forms — the ones used with Weckstrom's acryl — are cast by induction mold in a centrifuge and then hand-finished.

The result? An almost perfect harmony between contrasting materials. Acryl — almost as delicate as blown glass — grows out of sterling silver in such a way that the induced subtleties of color work to bleed the two materials together.

Ring.

Iron mold used for casting acryl
forms for Bjorn Weckstrom's silver-
acryl series. This mold is used for
one of the series pendants.

Powdered acryl is poured into the
"hopper" on the casting machine.

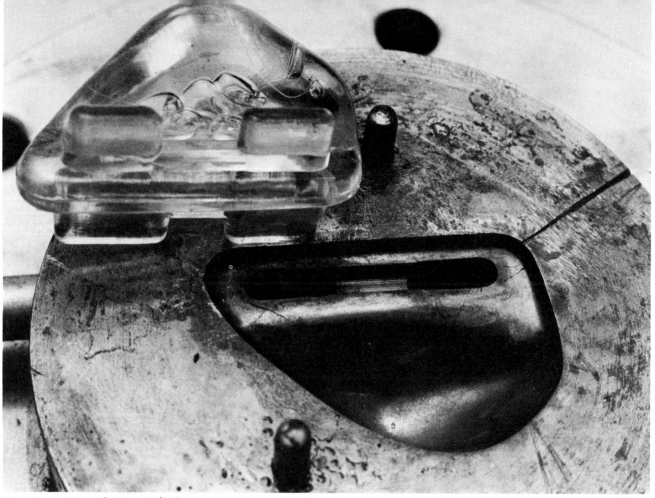

Rough acryl form (with mold) after
being cast.

Rough cast acryl form is filed and
trimmed.

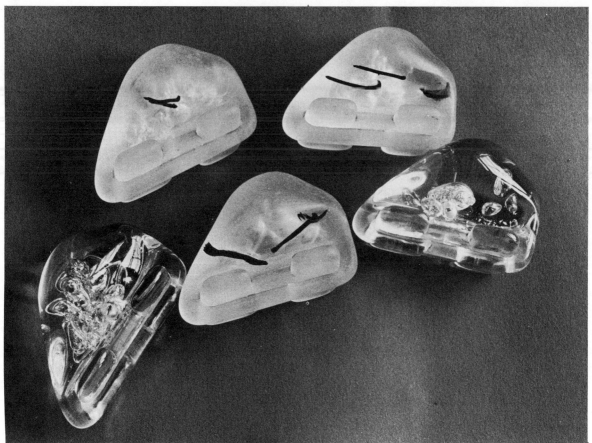

Acryl forms both before and after
they have been polished.

Color is injected into the acryl
form.

A three-part pendant is ready for
final cementing under pressure. Top
and bottom pieces are silver. Center
is acryl.

Stanley Lechtzin

United States

The term "electroforming" and the name Stanley Lechtzin have become almost synonymous. A few years ago, one might have dubbed electroforming an experimental technique, but not any more. Through his work, Stanley has become a master, rather than an experimenter.

Stanley's most recent energies have been directed toward adding to, and growing metal over cast polyester forms. His metal has very often become like a skin, or shell that surrounds an inner core of polyester. In other words, Stanley is concerned with what goes on outside of and around the plastic instead of with something going on inside the polyester.

Stanley's wife, Edith Lechtzin, has contributed this word picture about her "old man."

Stanley Lechtzin? Yes, a constant flow of ideas within a perpetually questioning mind. Blend this with a love of technology, motorcycles, airplanes, and other dangerous challenges, and there you have something of what makes up Stanley Lechtzin.

He works best in a hectic atmosphere of scheduled pressures, and does so within an ultra-organized workshop. He enjoys being loquacious and can talk at great length about his work, not to mention about contemporary metalwork in general.

He's a blend. A highly organized, logical mind mixed with the tastes and desires of a postpuberty adolescent male.

And when Stanley himself is backed up against a wall with pen in hand, he has this to say about his work:

I consider jewelry to be a three-dimensional art form with the function of embellishing the body. However, it should make a statement which can be appreciated in isolation.

Approximately ten years ago, I reached the point in my work where the structures I wished to create were no longer possible with traditional tools and techniques. I therefore began to explore the possibilities presented by our contemporary industrial technology. I found it possible, using the electroforming process, to develop relatively large-scale yet lightweight objects. Combinations of materials which were difficult or impossible to achieve were made feasible. In providing answers to immediate problems, electroforming has also opened form and structural possibilities which I would not have predicted before beginning my work in this technique.

I attempt to create personal values using materials and processes which today are used in a mechanical and anonymous manner by industry. The control which I exercise over the metal as it grows in the electrolytic solution is a source of stimulation. This process is analogous to numerous growth processes observed in nature, and this has considerable meaning for me. It brings to mind crystal growth, the growth of coral under the sea, and the multiplication of simple organisms as observed under the microscope. In this, I experience a relationship between technology and nature.

Recently I have been attracted to plastics because of their rich colors and marvelous transparencies. Here again, I enjoy utilizing in an intuitive manner a material that was developed for technological needs. The processes and materials which I employ require me to work in a methodical and logical manner, and I am sure this influences my structures. Yet the source of my forms must ultimately be ascribed to nature.

Torque of green polyester and electroformed silver gilt.

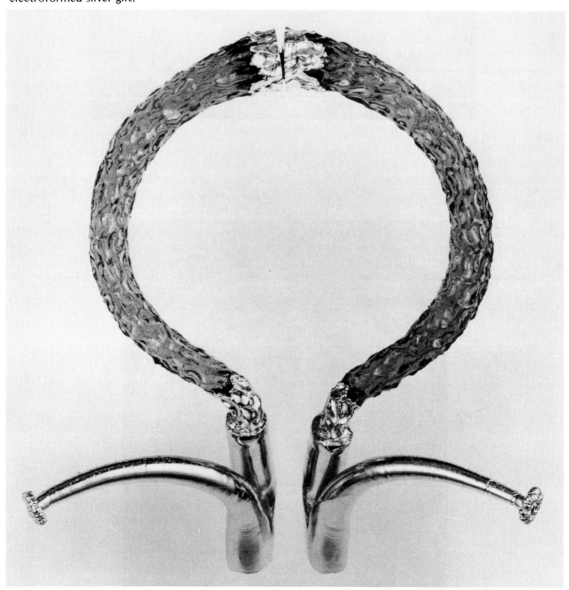

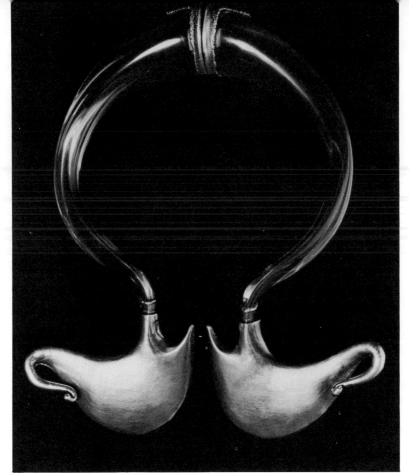

Torque of nut-brown polyester and
electroformed silver.

Torque of clear polyester and
electroformed copper.
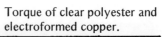

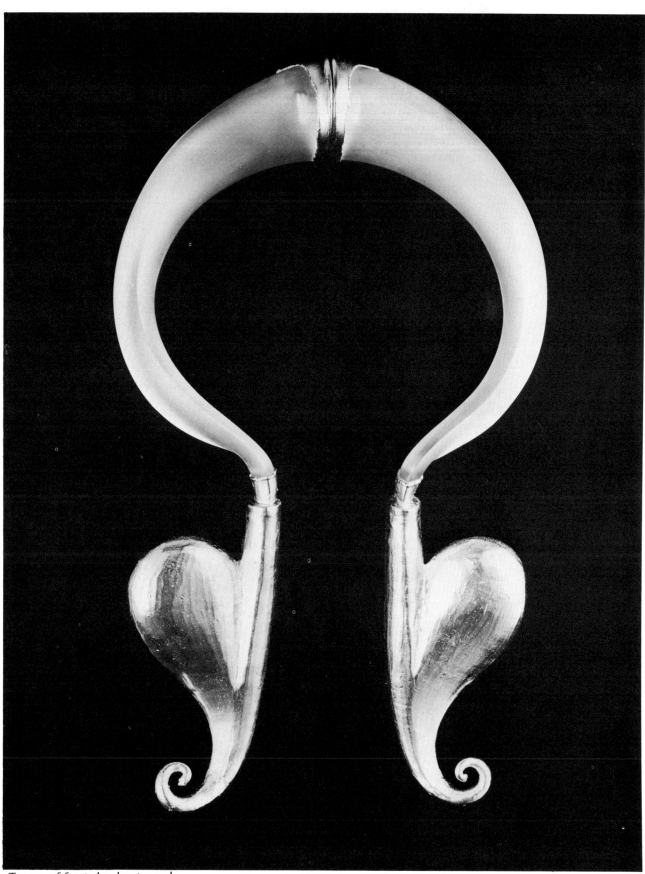

Torque of frosted polyester and
electroformed silver gilt.

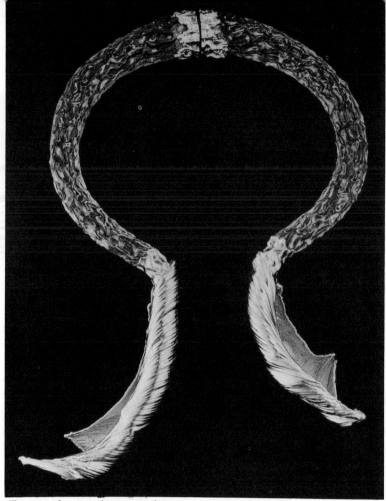

Torque of gray polyester and
electroformed silver gilt.

Torque of amber polyester and
electroformed silver.

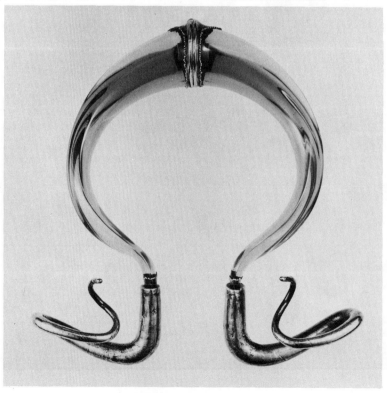

170

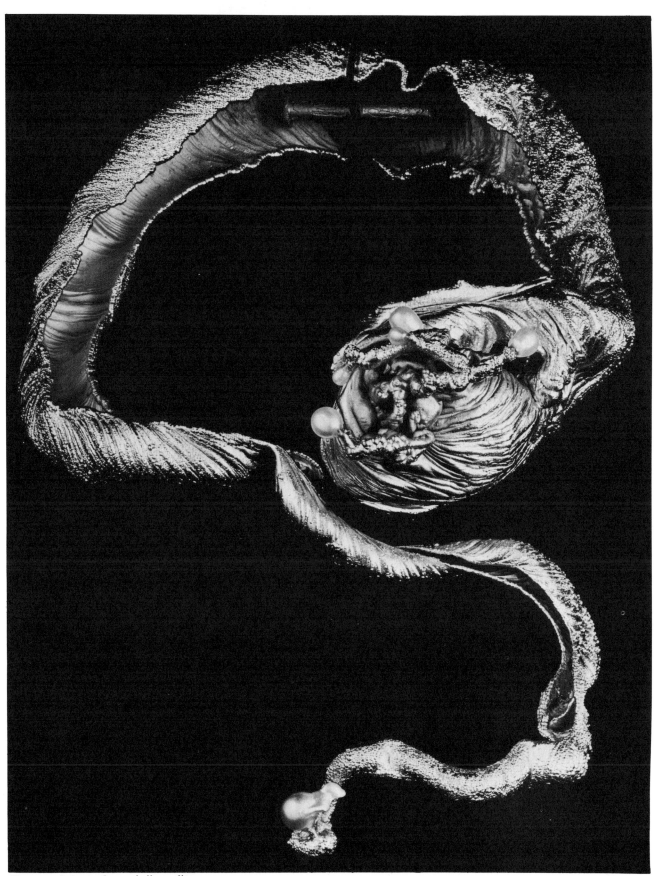

Torque of electroformed silver gilt
and pearls.

171

Bracelet of electroformed silver gilt with 2 moonstones.

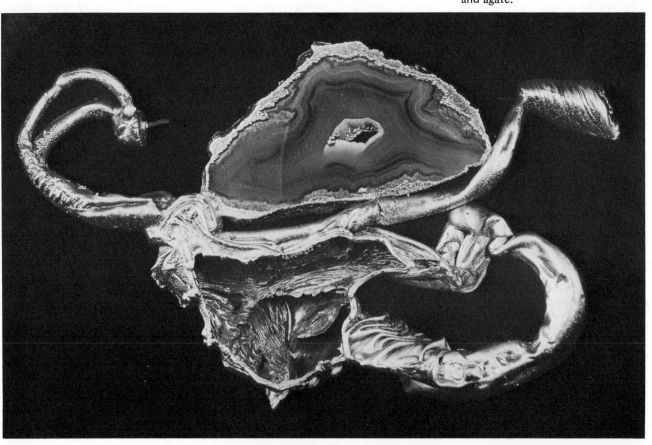

Brooch of electroformed silver gilt and agate.

Brooch of electroformed silver gilt
and quartz crystals.

Brooch of electroformed silver gilt
and amethyst crystal.

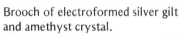

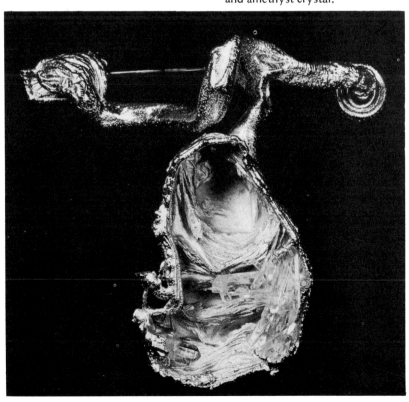

Eleanor Moty

United States

For the past several years Eleanor Moty has incorporated both photo-etching and photoelectroplating techniques within her jewelry forms. Her techniques involve the use of photography and photosensitive resists.

When she first began exploring these techniques, Eleanor used the photographic image as the main theme around which to build her forms. Later, as she dug a bit deeper into her technical possibilities, she turned toward using the photographic image as a surprise element within a design or as a visual focal point — somewhat in the same manner as one might use a stone. By means of photoetching or photoelectroplating she could repeat textures, patterns, and even form lines within her forms by superimposing these onto the jewel. Sometimes she even begins a jewel form by allowing a photo image to suggest what shape, surface, and texture the metal should take. Although Eleanor uses her photoetching and photoelectroplating techniques primarily on metal, she has also found they offer exciting possibilities for use on glass and ceramics.

Eleanor recently organized her thoughts and working procedures for a *Craft Horizons* article, from which some of the following material is taken (courtesy of the American Craftsmans Council).

To begin a simplified procedure for contact printing on flat metal sheets such as copper, silver, bronze, or gold, make sure the metal is completely clean before it is coated with photosensitive resist. The resist will not adhere to a surface filmed over with oil or oxides. Scrubbing the surface with a pumice and water slurry and then rinsing the metal thoroughly under cold water is the general recommended procedure for cleaning a surface. If the rinse water refuses to bead, or "break," on the metal surface, then the surface is considered chemically clean.

The clean metal plate is then dried, with either filtered forced air or an absorbent cloth. Once dry, it can be dipped in or sprayed with photosensitive resist. Photosensitive resists are light-sensitive, and therefore processing should be done under "safe" lights until the image is developed. The resist-coated metal plate must then either be dried in an air-circulating oven at no higher than 176 degrees F. for ten minutes or air-dried in a light-tight box for about twenty-four hours or longer, depending upon the outside temperature and humidity.

Several firms manufacture photosensitive resists as well as supply and instruction manuals on technical procedure. Many of these resists are manufactured for use on specific materials, and one must therefore follow closely the instructions supplied by the manufacturer. Eleanor has experienced positive results using the products and instruction manuals supplied by the Eastman Kodak Company of Rochester, New York.

For best results on metal, Eleanor recommends high-contrast transparencies — in other words, opaque black and clear acetate without gray tones. The transparency image must be sharp, preferably with dense black areas. Continuous tone images can be made into halftone, or can be made on a dot pattern resembling a coarse screen. An eighty-five- or sixty-line pattern is adequate.

A proper light source must be used for polymer resists. For her contact printing, Eleanor fitted four fifteen-watt unfiltered black lights into a hinged, covered metal box and then suspended a sheet of plate glass three inches above the fluorescent tubes in order to keep the exposure factor constant during the initial trial exposure. Eleanor cautions that care should be taken so as not to look directly into these unfiltered fluorescent lights — the ultraviolet rays are harmful.

To print the photo image on the photosensitive metal, the high-contrast transparency should be placed emulsion side up on the plate glass above the lights. The resist-coated metal is placed over the transparency and then a foam-rubber blanket or padding is placed over the metal, so that when the lid of the box is closed a tight contact is made between the metal and the transparency. Eleanor uses a ten-minute exposure with her own light box. In order to develop the transparency image on the photosensitive metal, she gently agitates the metal in a tray of recommended photo resist developer for one to two minutes and then rinses the metal in a spray of cool water.

The developers themselves act as solvents for the photo resists. When an exposure is made, light reaches areas of metal not protected by black (opaque) areas on the transparency. When the resist is exposed to light, it polymerizes and forms a resistant coating, which "insulates" it from the developer, etchants, and plating baths. Unexposed areas of resist dissolve in the developer and are washed away. This results in the exposed raw metal for etching or plating.

After being developed, the resist image must be baked on the metal surface for ten minutes at temperatures ranging from 210 to 250 degrees Fahrenheit, depending upon the photo resist being used. This baking makes the resist more durable. Care should be taken not to bake at excessive temperatures. Excessive baking may cause the resist to become brittle and to break down during further processing.

At this point the metal is ready for etching or electroplating. The manuals recommend specific mordants for various metals. Eleanor has found that a 40-60 nitric acid-water mordant is suitable for silver, copper, and bronze. While working, it is important to agitate the etchant. This allows for an even, efficient etching, especially when the image has fine detail or is a halftone dot pattern. Etching must be watched carefully. Timing depends upon the strength of the mordant and upon how deep into the surface the etching is made. It is possible to etch only as deep as the width of a line or a dot, since undercutting occurs and image sharpness can eventually disappear.

In most cases, greater image depth can be achieved through plating. This also allows the introduction of a contrasting metal such as silver or copper onto the base. If the image is to be electroplated after baking, then metals such as copper and silver should be dipped in a 10 percent solution of ammonium persulphate for from thirty seconds to one minute. This solution acts as a mild etchant on the exposed metal. Ordinarily, metal is electrocleaned in an alkaline solution prior to plating. This procedure, however, lifts the resist and should not be used. From this point forward, conventional heavy plating procedures can be followed.

After etching or plating is completed, the resist can be removed by soaking the metal in the stripper or solvent recommended by the manufacturer. The finished plate must not be worked or shaped with steel tools. An electroplated surface can lift or peel if the metal is distorted. For this reason, the finished plate should be used flat within the overall jewel form.

Eleanor has recently attempted to expose images by projecting them onto three-dimensional or previously formed, rather than flat, surfaces. This allows for more dimensionally proportioned jewelry. As the photo image is projected onto the formed metal surface, it has a tendency to distort in a way which Eleanor feels relates visually to the overall form.

Many resists require a projection system within an ultraviolet range such as xenon. Several others however, including "Kodak Ortho Resist," have wider spectral range, and can be exposed with tungsten light sources. A Kodak 850 carousel projector equipped with a 500-watt halogen bulb will, for example, expose "KOR" resist on metals such as bronze and copper.

The initial preparation of the metal for projection exposure is the same as that for contact printing except that two thin coats of resist may be necessary, allowing drying time between coats. The exposure factor must be recalculated because the distance from the light source to the object can change depending upon the photo images used. It is advisable to place the object as close as possible to the light source. High-contrast transparencies can be placed in slide mounts for projection printing. In this way, one image, when projected, can accommodate either small or large objects.

When one is focusing the image onto the metal, a filter must be placed in front of the lens to avoid fogging the photo resist. The filter used should correspond to the spectral range to which the resist is sensitive. If a filter is not used, focusing should be done on a substitute model, rather than on the actual resist-coated metal. The exposure can then be made on the resist-coated object. At a distance of three feet, a thirty-second to two-minute exposure is generally required, depending upon the quality of the image. The image should be in sharp focus on the frontal area of the object. As the image falls back into depressions and around edges, ellipses are formed by the dot pattern. Although areas out of focus will have incomplete exposure, it is possible to mask or cover up the frontal area so that the remainder of the image can be exposed for a longer period. As the light reflects against the metal, it may cause fogging. In order to reduce this possibility, it is advisable to use short exposures rather than long exposures for projection printing. After the exposure, the image should be developed for one to two minutes in a tray or container. The object is then processed for etching or plating in the manner described for contact printing.

Projection printing is more difficult than contact printing, and Eleanor has had only limited success with it. With projection printing, the resist tends to break down in the electroplating baths, and this causes only a minimal depth of image into the metal.

About her use of materials and her imagery Eleanor has this to say.

I am not particularly concerned about using materials with so-called intrinsic value. On the contrary, my choice of materials is purely visual. I tend more toward using slab agates, rough minerals, crystals, glass, found objects, and even copper and bronze.

Land and landscapes influence my forms either directly or intuitively. Earth formations, linear movement, and color tend to dictate my choice of materials, and occasionally even dictate my choice of photo images. Aside from the total visual imagery of my work, I employ secret or hidden images known only to me. Some of these secrets are eventually discovered; others are not. But that doesn't matter. It's the thought that counts! Does that make sense?

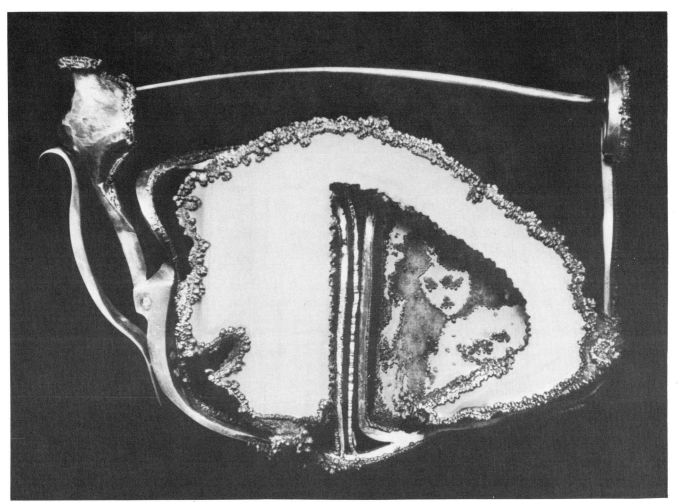

"Cameo" pin. Fabricated silver and 14-carat gold with copper photo-electroplate and agate.

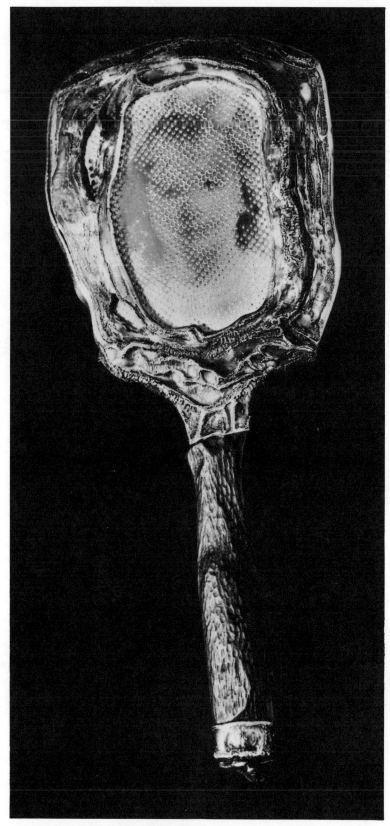

"Portrait" mirror. Fabricated silver
with silver photoelectroplate and
rosewood handle.

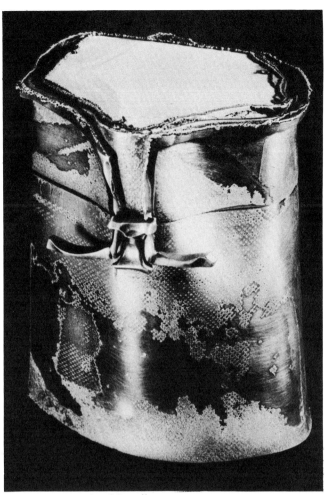

"Dodge City School Box."
Fabricated silver with silver photo-
electroplate and agate.

"Commemorative Box." Fabricated
silver with copper photo-
electroplate, photo-etched mirror,
and glass lens.

David Laplantz
United States

David Laplantz is one among us who quite obviously smiles and even laughs out loud through his forms. His technical craftsmanship is so meticulous that one almost feels that David's forms are thumbing their nose at perfection or at technology. It's as if David were saying. "To hell with super technology. Even I can become so technically competent that I can create forms that are perfect, but useless." Are David's forms jewelry? Or are they mini antisculptures? And who is it that defines the limits of a jewel?

Metal to me is like an extension of my own skin — a way for new life to begin. The excitement I feel in seeing the growth and development of each piece is beyond my ability to put it into words! I like to play with many different kinds of materials in my pieces. I most often work on many objects at once — something like from four to six pieces at the same time. In this way, when I tire of one I can go on to another. Often parts from one piece will work better on one of the other pieces, so I switch them around. In this way, I can stop that stagnant sickness often occurring in art.

Each piece is always new and different — no two being exactly alike, each with a life of its own. I like to have fun when I'm working with metal, just as when I'm teaching. There is no division between the two. They seem to blend together. Each is a groping, a search for knowledge, and each has an end — a finished metal object, whether it turns out to be a toy, something to wear, or whatever. Each is an object with sensual feelings to me, tactile all over, something a person without eyesight might fully enjoy. Metal speaks if one has time to stop, to listen, to feel, and to experience either the joy or the sorrow the maker felt. I am happy in metal — what more can one ask for? It fulfills a deep desire. I do it and feel refreshed.

On other matters, I think it's too bad folks get the way they do about things like the right way to talk about crafts, or world history, or whatever! The world of crafts often really turns me off — you get those big guns who think they are so fantastic but who have not worked for years. Then, there are the craft houses which want tons of percents and dollars; and, of course, the weird publishing business that rewrites stuff or just plain screws you.

Engraved raised and forged brass
"Sick Rattle." 6½ inches high.

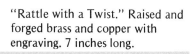

"Rattle with a Twist." Raised and
forged brass and copper with
engraving. 7 inches long.

"Long If You Like It That Way." Sculptural playtoy to "shake, rattle, or roll." It has a spring on the tail so that the individual round discs have movement. There are small loose bearings inside the form tube, which rattle. 16 inches long.

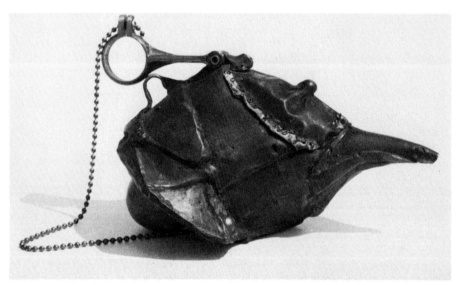

"Anteater Vacuum Cleaner." Cast brass with formed brass sewn to top section in front of ring. The base is a leather ball. 8 inches long.

Sterling silver wine container. Raised, forged, and fabricated silver. 6 inches long.

"Burroughs Carriage Return Number 3." Made from leather, brass, found objects, and parts from an old typewriter. It incidentally functions as a small container, but also has a sort of "feelie" quality for getting, as David puts it, "turned on" from the physical play with its surfaces. 7 inches long.

"Burroughs Carriage Return Number 3," second view.

Richard Mawdsley

United States

Well, here it is! My art history teacher once told me that I wrote like a third-grader, and that if I didn't marry a smart girl, I'd end up in deep trouble.

My jewelry forms are attempts on my part to interpret and to visualize the significant events I have experienced and the objects associated with those events. I also place these "visualizations" into images that I feel are significant to the American scene of the 1970s.

As an artist, I find my images and personal temperament seem to come out most successfully in jewelry forms and in precious and semiprecious materials. Also, I simply like to work with my hands. These materials allow me to do so, and at the same time the precious materials allow me to make beautiful little things — hopefully beautiful little significant things.

I am pushed to create, to explore, to build because if I don't do so, my role as a teacher, an educated man, husband, father, and member of this culture will be meaningless. Most of all I do it because I simply like to.

Jewelry can be anything. Only the individual who wears the form can decide if the object is a jewel. If the potential wearer doesn't want to call the object "jewelry," then he doesn't have to wear it. I feel that the world is loosening up to what forms personal adornment can take. I believe we have gone through a period in history in which there were very tight bounds on what a significant jewel could be. I call this period and these jewels "creative decoration." I believe that in my culture, at least in my own case, there is a renewed interest in jewelry history and the forms significant to historical periods. Through renewed interest, I have learned that jewelry can be large, sumptuous, bold, aggressive, and be a very meaningful symbol of man's relationship to his society.

"Queen Bee." Pin in sterling silver with jade and pearls. The head was cast, but the remainder was fabricated from wire, tubing, and sheet.

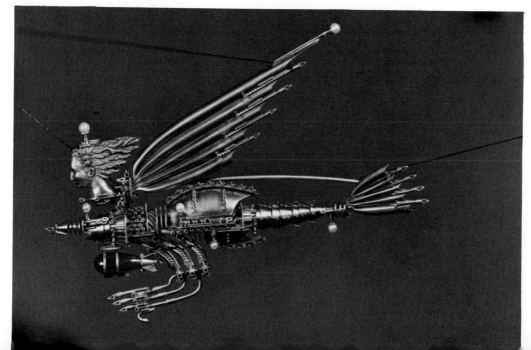

184

"The Red Baron." Pendant in
sterling silver, lapis lazuli, and
garnets. Fabricated with cast head.
The idea came from "an early love
of model airplanes."

Ken Cory
United States

Ken Cory is yet another in the growing number of jewelry craftsmen whose forms have turned the tables on traditional definitions. Most of Ken's work is small, having no more than a maximum dimension of 1-3/4 inches. He works mostly with nonprecious materials, often contrasting several materials and techniques within the same piece. Ken contributes the following words.

Jewelry is first of all sculpture. My primary concern is the idea behind the piece. Design follows idea.

My sculptures are not made to decorate the body, but because of their size they may be conveniently displayed on the body. The pieces are functional only to the extent that they are not too heavy to wear — there are no sharp points to stab the wearer, and they are durable. Too many jewelers let concept suffer in favor of function.

My jewelry is sculpture complete in itself wherever it is displayed. It can be worn by men or women. It can be hung on the wall like tiny portable sculpture. Too many artists think importance and volume are directly proportional.

All people throughout time have thought basically the same thoughts. They have been aware of the same mysteries and the same magic. As their environments vary, so do their languages. We have a visual language as well as a verbal one. In my jewelry, I am translating into contemporary visual language the thoughts of ancient cultures, which are, of course, the same thoughts we are thinking today. I make jewelry for the same reasons that the Egyptians built pyramids, the alchemists worked in their laboratories, and the Chinese wrote the *I-Ching*.

I try to ignore the monetary value of materials. I work predominantly in nonprecious materials, but I do not ignore the precious ones. Why not set a diamond in plastic, or combine gold and lead in the same piece? Tradition should neither be worshiped nor rejected.

I do not exclude from consideration any combinations of materials, techniques, or thoughts. Every teacher I've had has said that copper cannot be cast. So I tried it, and found that it could be cast. It does have limitations, but what material, technique, or thought doesn't? The artist's function is not to produce objects, but to produce objects as a demonstration or communication of his spiritual awareness.

Pin. Cast copper base with silver levers set with cornelians protruding through a brass plate bolted down with miniature brass bolts. The copper was oxidized into a wood-brown color. The texture results from casting the base from a balsa wood model.

Copper pin cast from a balsa wood and plastic model. The piece was then partially filled with polyester casting resin. The copper under the plastic is protected from the atmosphere — thus preserving its bright surface — while the outer surface has tarnished naturally.

Copper pin cast from balsa wood with brass plates and lever. Lever top is from bone.

Reversible pin. The piece is virtually the same on both sides. It is made from fabricated brass, agates, leather, and a standard safety pin.

J. Fred Woell

United States

J. Fred Woell, both in words and in form, has a bear hug way of reaching us all — and often reaching us right at our most sensitive spot. In his own very special way J. Fred Woell is the personification of all of us. Whether or not we agree with his work and what he says, we must at least admit that we share vibrant blood with him.

Give J. Fred Woell a "truth," axiom, or a slice of irrefutable logic and he'll not only tear it to bits, but he'll do it in his own gentle, half-satirical, half-humorous way without severing our blood ties with him. It is no small task to expose humanity raw, and to still keep its friendship and love. But J. Fred Woell does it.

His letterhead stationery contains a drawing of a bull. This bull wears a cattle brand: a star. Under the brand, he has printed the word "artist," but the word is printed so that it falls over onto its side, along with the words "J. Fred Woell."

J. Fred's forms are pulled straight out from the guts of the culture he knows. He translates something of America into every object he makes, into the way he uses materials, and into his way of expressing these materials.

I am not an artist or a craftsman. I am at best someone who enjoys working with his hands, or in other words, enjoys making things. I've never really been able to get into jewelry or metalsmithing in the way a true professional does. I generally learn what I want to of a technique or process just in order to make what I have in mind. Of course, there is more to it than all that. Nothing has quite that simple an explanation. I do make a lot of jewelry, and I suppose that's why my work is being included in this book. But I seldom make work for people, and when I do, I'm so damned frustrated by the time I'm through that I'm a nervous wreck.

I'll never be a successful professional. As soon as I get onto something that is successful or popular (or whatever you want to call it), I find myself finished with it and ready to move onto something else. I guess that's because each thing I make (whether it's worth repeating or not), is a very personal and singular statement in itself. There are those moments when I'm in the mood to make frivolous things and I do so. There are other times when I want to tell the world where to get off and I try and scream it out through my work. I enjoy a good laugh and I particularly enjoy satire. I try to bring a sense of humor to my work and I hope it shows.

Despite what I say, I'd still like to be successful at what I do and have people like my work. It doesn't seem very likely that I deserve either, especially considering my own attitude. I guess that's why I understand when people don't like my work, despite my wish that they would. All of this really does seem to make sense to me, especially when one considers the world of creativity (the world of art, the artists, or whatever you want to call it). Which reminds me of a sign I read in a store the other day:

I know you believe you understand
what you think I said, but I am not sure
that you realize what you heard is not
what I meant.

Life is a joke — a bad joke. My work is like that — a bad joke. It
ain't funny, but it makes fun of this bad joke — life. Oh yes, you
may say to me, "Look how lucky you are, you've got everything: good
health, talent, a chance to make something out of yourself — so why
be bitter? Why look at the gloomy side?" And I must admit that you're
right. I am lucky. I can add to that "success list" that I am
protestant, white, without a particular axe to grind, that I blend
in, I get along, and I don't seem to feel the need for rocking the
boat.

Life is still a bad joke no matter how you cut it. Man never at
any time has lived in peace, nor has he ever been able to accept his
fellow men as they come to him, without some preconditioned
prejudice. Race, creed, color divide us, separate us, and inhibit our
freedom.

Nothing is precious to man. We waste. We have little respect for
anything. The waters are polluted. The air is polluted. Nature has
been raped by our greed. Our endless orgy leaves its scars along
every inch of our path.

Man is a disaster. We can't save ourselves. So we laugh and make fun
of our plight. It's a bad joke, but we laugh and somehow it lessens
the pain. And I join in the telling of it. The bad joke. It's the
humor in my work. It ain't funny, but somehow it helps. It helps
me feel a little better. And I can go on at least a little longer
without feeling the pain quite so much.

Here's my epilogue. I do not consider myself or my creative work
particularly unique. I am not a self-made artist. My aesthetic values
are an assemblage of ideas, influences, and images that are
continually crossing my path. My work is at best an eclectic statement
with little or no innovation of style, technique, or materials. I am
satisfied to leave such areas to others for development and perfection.
It is my purpose to learn what they know only insofar as it gives
me the facility to express myself adequately.

Scholarship is not my interest. Scholarship in itself is a dead end.
My curiosity centers more in knowing myself. I am self-centered, and
from this center comes the reason for my creating.

It is my aim to make an object look complete and possess a quality
that gives the work a presence or life of its own. And in doing so,
I try hard to keep the freshness of my fingerprint on the work and
to maintain an intimate, spontaneous quality that hopefully will
give it a timeless character.

"B. for Buffalo." Pin detaches from
frame. Cast silver.

190

"Now That the Buffalo's Gone."
Pendant in bronze, brass, and silver.

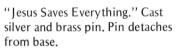

"Jesus Saves Everything." Cast
silver and brass pin. Pin detaches
from base.

"Requiem for a President." Pin cast
in brass.

"November 22, 1963; 12:30 P.M."
Badge in copper, silver, brass, and
glass. Badge detaches from frame.

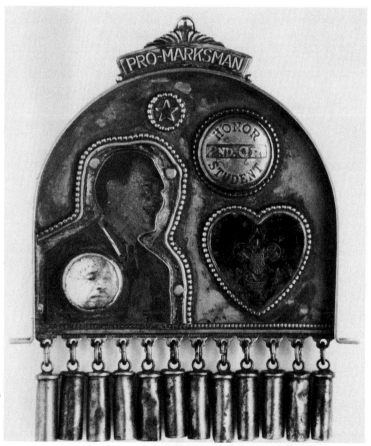

"The American Way." Badge in
copper, brass, silver. According to
J. Fred, it also contains a bit of
"etceteras."

"R.F.K. for President." Detaches
from frame. Badge in steel, copper,
silver, and glass.

"Great American Themes: The Only Good Indian Is a Dead Indian." Pendant in brass, bronze, silver, and copper.

"Whatever Happened to What's Her Name?" Badge in silver, steel, bronze, and glass.

"Requiem." Pin in silver, bronze, and glass. Pin detaches from frame.

"Patriotism Medal." Pendant in brass, copper, silver, glass, and steel.

Poul Havgaard
Denmark

Poul Havgaard's forms in iron are deliberate, nonaccidental sculptures. Poul builds his forms from a painstaking technique of "flowing," or welding drops of iron thread one upon another.

Although iron form can be built by casting, forging, and by electric welding, Poul prefers the acetylene torch. His torch technique using drops of melted thread is somewhat similar to the way in which nature forms stalagmites from drops of calcareous water. Poul has chosen the acetylene torch technique because it not only provides maximum form-building possibilities, but also allows for infinite precision and maximum control. With drops of melted iron, he is able to build both vertically and horizontally. Or he can build solids and even shell-like or skeletal hollow forms. By varying the thickness of his iron thread, he can vary the size of his liquid iron drops.

Poul feels that, even though many craftsmen have tried building iron forms from electric welding, the electric arc technique is just too cumbersome for refined, precision mini-form. Electric welding normally requires the use of a face mask and very heavy insulated gloves. Acetylene welding, on the other hand, requires only special glasses. Poul feels that the need to wear a face mask and gloves places the artist too far away from his work. It reduces the intimacy between artist, material, and form and results in too many physical working inconveniences — dragging cords, adjusting temperature controls, lifting and lowering a mask, and removing and replacing thick gloves.

The form-building process between acetylene and electric welding is also quite different. Whereas acetylene welding is a kind of spontaneous growing of iron, electric welding involves more of an assembly process, a seaming together of parts — often parts with broad seams because of the technique. Poul is not opposed to electric welding — he just feels it is more suited to large sculptural forms than to jewelry.

On many of his forms, Poul begins from a flat surface — a small disc or scrap of iron plate cut or burned out to the approximate base shape of his eventual form. From this base, he then builds almost organically, drop by welded drop. Heat control and a steady, even placement of droplets are both essential elements of his technique. Too much heat will "float" the form away; too little heat causes erratic building and especially unwanted "pits." As he builds, Poul trys to keep as close to his final form as possible. The more exact he is, the less he will have to reduce or grind away later. When reducing is necessary, he uses either hand files or a heavy duty electric drill with either sanding heads or grinding bits. When the final form has been reached and refined by sanding, Poul dips the iron in cutting oil, lights the oil, and allows the oil to burn on the iron, producing an oxidized, blackened surface. He then polishes the form surfaces, but only those surfaces he wants colored silver. The remaining surfaces are left untouched. The result is a contrast between blackened concavities, and polished, silverlike top surfaces. The final step is to dip the forms into or brush them with a two-component (binder plus hardener) transparent polyester lacquer to prevent rusting.

Poul often combines his iron forms with leather — iron buckles with leather belts, iron jewels on handbag flaps, iron pendants on leather body forms, and even iron buttons growing on leather and fur garments. On many of his forms, he also sets beachstones such as flint — or he may set amber, amethyst, or fossils, or even weld in contrasting surfaces of brass.

The Danish reception of Poul's iron forms has been a complete back-to-front experience. His forms were literally rejected by every jewelry medium considered holy in Denmark. For a long while he was not even invited to exhibit his iron in his own country, nor was he given a single word of coverage in the two Danish handcraft and design magazines.

Perhaps part of the reason for his Danish rejection is that Poul is a maverick and has never pressed himself within the tight clique of critics, authority figures, and other jewelry craftsmen who hold absolute rein on the Danish jewelry scene. After rejection by every Danish crafts resource, he turned to Paris and to Pierre Cardin. Cardin immediately recognized the value of Poul's work, bought many exclusive collections, and featured Poul's iron at one of his major international fashion shows in Paris. Only then, after Poul had made his own way outside of Denmark, was his work finally noticed at home.

At the beginning of the 1970s, Poul was invited to join Kruunu Koru of Finland. The idea was that he should come up with a new collection of forms that could be produced in silver on a multiple-series basis. He was not to become a Kruunu Koru factory employee. On the contrary, he was invited to work in his own studio, on his own terms, and contract the sale of his prototypes for mass production on a royalty basis. This proved to be an ideal working arrangement for both industry and the independent craftsman.

Poul built his prototypes from iron — the material he was comfortable with technically, and the material in which he felt he could best express his feeling for form. The prototypes were much larger and much bolder than traditional series forms in silver. Many of them had moving parts — in other words, one could change the whole form composition by rotating the individual parts. The prototype pendants, for example, were made so that as the pendant rested against the body, the composition could rotate by virtue of the movable parts. Kruunu Koru accepted thirty of these first iron prototypes and agreed to produce them in silver on a multiple-series basis.

Thus began the painstaking process of converting bold, technically complicated rotating iron prototypes into silver — and doing so without abusing the integrity of form that Poul had captured in iron. The first step was to take a full, three-dimensional impression of the iron forms in silicone rubber. Each iron form was completely submerged in a container of semi-paste, semiliquid silicone. Kruunu Koru craftsmen had to be very certain that the silicone filled every crevice and contour of the original prototype form. At this point the silicone was vulcanized and then allowed to "stabilize," or harden, around the iron. The stabilized silicone was then removed from around the iron in two matching halves. With this process completed, the craftsmen now had a first rubber mold to use in eventual silver conversion.

The next step was to place the two halves of the silicone mold back together, secure the halves, and then, with injection under pressure, fill the mold with melted impression wax. But before this could be done, a tiny trench or injection groove had to be carved in the rubber — a trench through which the wax could be injected into the mold after the mold halves were secured together.

This process of injecting wax into the silicone mold had to be controlled carefully. Normally, one could just fill the mold up with wax to gain an exact positive, but Kruunu Koru was not after a *solid* wax positive. They wanted a hollow or shell-like positive in order to conserve the quantity of silver being used for each large form. To gain hollow positive, the silicone mold had to be only partially wax filled and then rotated so that the wax could run around on the inside of the mold, covering all mold surfaces evenly without glopping up into a solid. It was necessary to repeat this step many times before a correct wax positive was gained. The minimum thickness of the wax positive walls had to be kept at 0.6 millimeters. From previous experience, they had found that walls thinner than 0.6 millimeters were just too flimsy and often caused "pitting" or "pocking" of the form surfaces.

After the wax positive on each form was perfected, the positive was placed on (and fused with) a round wax stand or pedestal. The stand was placed in a base, and a tubelike container was built around both the wax positive and the round wax stand. This whole container was then filled with "gyps," or casting plaster, and set on a vibrator to force the plaster to fill evenly and to produce a perfect negative of the wax positive.

After the plaster had hardened, the plaster was heated just enough to melt the wax positive. This melted wax then escaped from the plaster mold through the negative space left by the round wax stand or pedestal. Because the wax positive had in itself been hollow, the resultant plaster mold also produced a hollow or shell-like controlled form.

The plaster mold was then placed in a centrifuge, and the silver was "cast" into the mold by centrifugal force. The rings in the series required two separate casting molds — one for the band and one for the top form. Some of the other larger hanging pieces required as many as three or four separate castings in order to build the whole form. The cast pieces were refined by hand and then assembled (soldered) together into completed form.

On the pendants for the series, Poul discovered how to control the placement of the forms on the body. He wanted the forms down and away from the neck. He wanted them framed by the breasts and by a less interrupted surface than one normally encounters with collars, garment openings, buttons, and necklines. To drop the forms lower onto the breast, he built them from long, thin slivers of metal that grew organically. This "teardrop" form-building technique even helped to override the limitations of the more or less standardized neck chains used on serial pieces. By means of the long, thin metal sliver, he visually separated the form from the neck chain.

When the series collection was introduced, Kruunu Koru excelled even in so far as advertising and packaging. For example, each silver jewel came packaged in a delicate silver drawstring bag with a white, furlike lining. Not bad! Especially when one compares a Kruunu Koru form to most of the other industrial guck flooding the jewelry markets today.

Havgaard's latest forms for series production in silver were again made in iron prototype. These are mini-forms that can be added or built onto a base form by threading components together. The idea, for example, is that one can buy an inexpensive basic silver ring and then later buy one or several additional parts to the ring, which can be threaded onto the basic form to build a whole new composition or one of several interchangeable compositions. His technique of contrasting polished surfaces against oxidized, blackened surfaces allows him to completely conceal the threading hole in the black surfaces of the basic form.

Iron jewelry? Yes! With nothing more than the most common of all non-precious metals, Havgaard has managed to cause many redefinitions of weary truisms. About himself, his work, and his medium, Poul has this to say.

I don't spend much time thinking about other people's jewelry. What I mean is that most of it is so void of meaning that it doesn't give me anything to think about or even react to. Too much of today's jewelry is undangerous. The scene is sweet, but it has no meaning.

I feel that too many jewelry designers have become political, and when they become political their forms also become political. By political, I mean in the sense of a modern politician — the message is biteless, gutless, and it echoes only hot air and catch phrases.

How does one become dangerous or meaningful? Well, a good place to begin is just to be honest. All materials — even a dog turd — can be potentially dangerous if they are used in a meaningful way. Jewelry is something other than the accumulation of precious materials. People say that my forms are dangerous because they provoke by their size, their materials, and their soul.

Every piece of jewelry is a form — a piece of mini-sculpture — and, as such, it is subject to the same rules of space and relationships as a painting or a piece of sculpture. Too many craftsmen ignore or never even learn the rules of giving birth to form. They walk always outside the sculptural considerations, and their forms show it. A strong form can't be an accident. A good form is always deliberate. The maker knows exactly where he is going. When I set a stone in iron, for example, I often carry the stone around in my pocket for a week, just to feel it, to understand it, and to know where I must go before I set the stone. It works! That stone and I communicate.

All of us who make form today are subject to the pressures of a plastic world — a world which stands and dictates to us how we must be, conceive, and think. A jewelry designer should stand outside this plastic world, just as a sculptor or a painter must. He should be an innovator rather than a follower.

Exhibitions? They exhaust me. Making money? I don't know much about it. I think it's as difficult as hell. Yes, I'd like to make some money, but only without making compromises.

Craft books? Well, the way of trying to write a do-it-yourself crafts book would be all right if it worked, but I think the times and thousands of existing books have pretty much indicated that there must be a better way.

What to say to young people? Well, I used to believe in young people. But today young people seem to be young only until they are about twenty, and then, just as quickly as they fall within the machinery of the adult world, they become just like everybody else. The ideals disappear. This is depressing indeed.

Most of the time when people come to ask my opinion or to interview me for the newspapers they seem to expect me to give what they call negative answers. I've been pretty much labeled as a giver of negative answers. Sometimes I feel like these journalists look at me and say to themselves: "Who does he think he is — some kind of a god?" If they aren't thinking along those lines, then they think I'm some kind of a clown. And I am.

It's become the symbol of safety to say nothing. When I react in the way other people label negative, I do so as a positive gesture. It's my way of saying that changes must be made, that problems must be solved, and that we cannot live forever in a world of plastic people.

Adjustable iron and leather breast pendant.

Iron and leather breast pendant, second view.

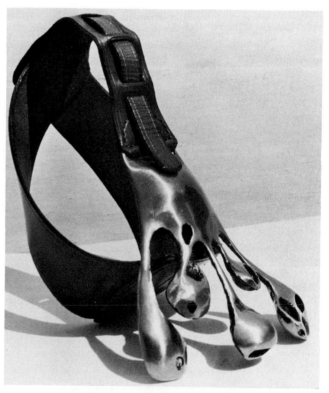

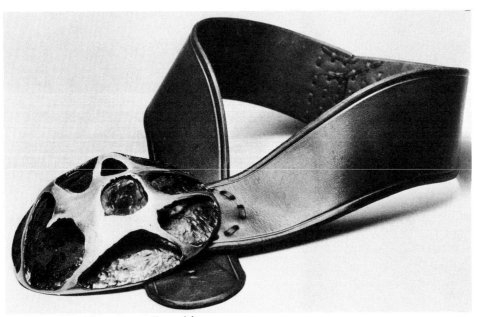

Iron buckle with raw cornelian with
leather belt.

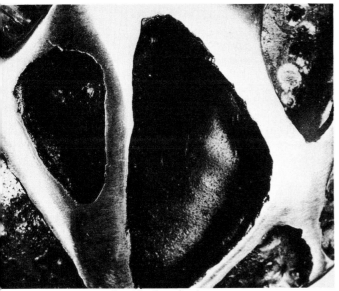

Detail of iron buckle. Iron background has been burned with oil to
oxidize it black.

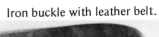

Iron buckle with leather belt.

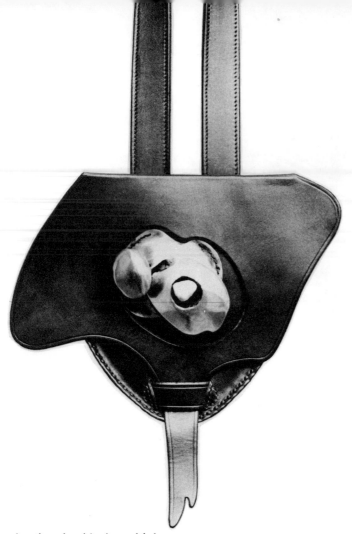

Leather shoulder bag with iron
jewel.

Detail, leather shoulder bag with
iron jewel.

Detail, iron jewel.

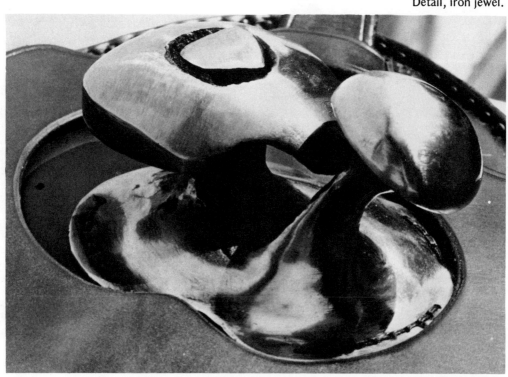

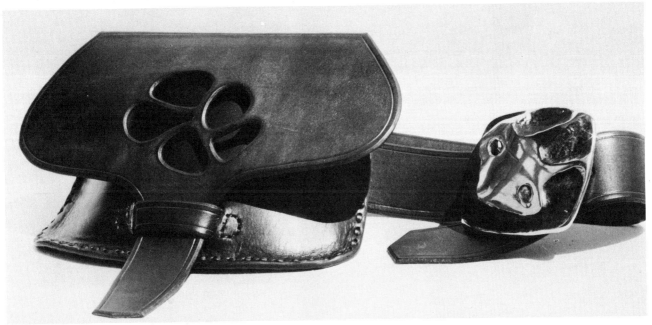

Leather belt bag with cast zinc
buckle.

Leather shoulder bag with iron
jewel.

Leather shoulder bag with iron
jewel.

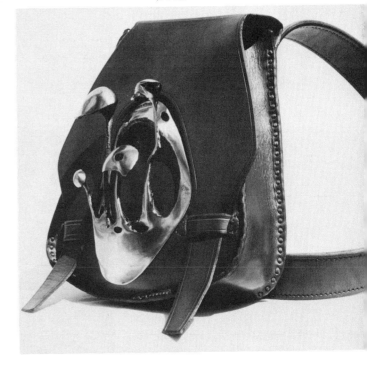

Iron ring with burned and oxidized
surfaces.

To begin an iron ring, Poul first
carried this piece of amber around
in his pocket for a week, just to feel
and understand the personality of
the stone.

He begins a form by burning out a
small base plate with the oxygen-
acetylene tip on the torch.

With an iron thread or rod, plus the torch, he begins forming walls around the iron base plate — drop by drop.

As the iron setting is built, it occasionally needs to be ground down to allow for a perfect fit.

The amber with the growing form.

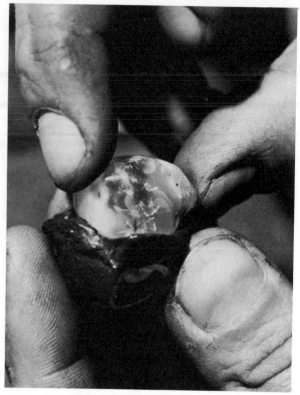

The amber begins to fit snugly
into the iron.

The iron gradually grows around
the amber.

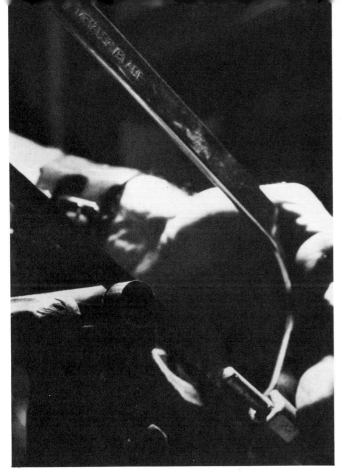

The ring band is cut from a length of iron pipe.

The rough-sawed ring band is placed on the setting, bottom side up.

With drops of iron thread, the rough-sawed ring band is welded to the iron setting.

207

Ring band and setting become one.

The amber fits snugly into the form. Front view after the iron has been dipped in oil, burned, and oxidized.

Second view of ring after oxidizing.

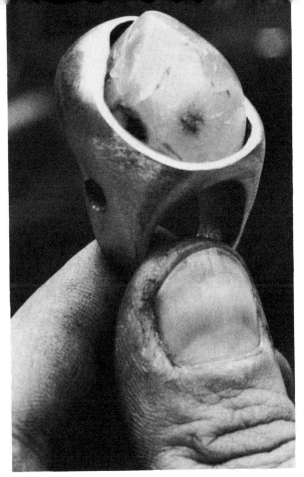

The final ring before the amber is
cemented in place. Outer iron
surfaces have been polished to a
silver color.

The final ring, second view.

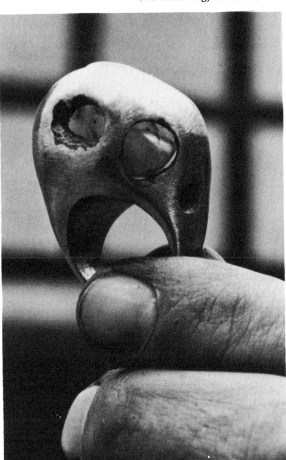

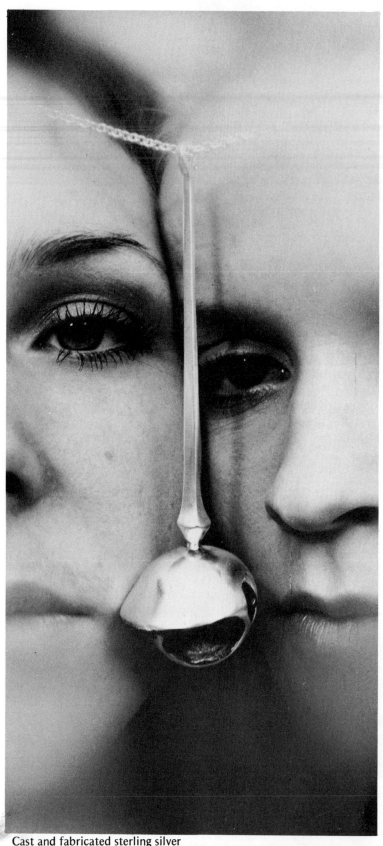

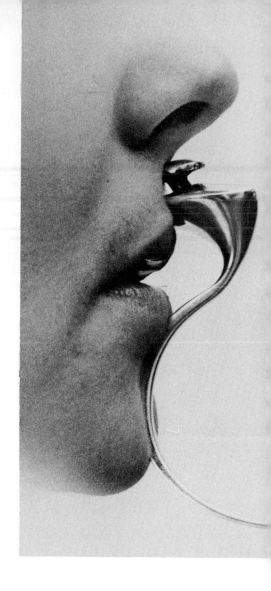

Cast and fabricated sterling silver
armband from iron prototype.

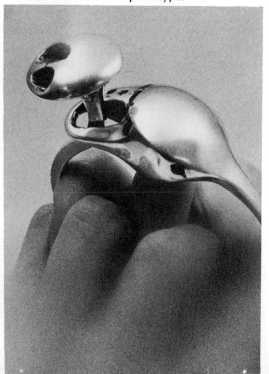

Cast and fabricated sterling silver
pendant with movable base. Cast
from iron prototype.

210

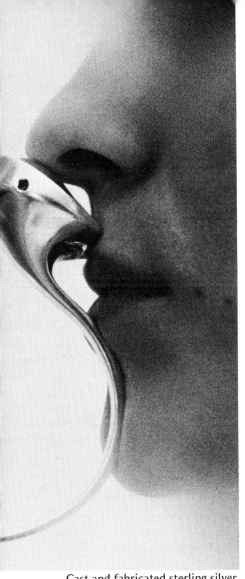

Cast and fabricated sterling silver
armband from iron prototype.

Cast and fabricated sterling silver
armband from iron prototype.

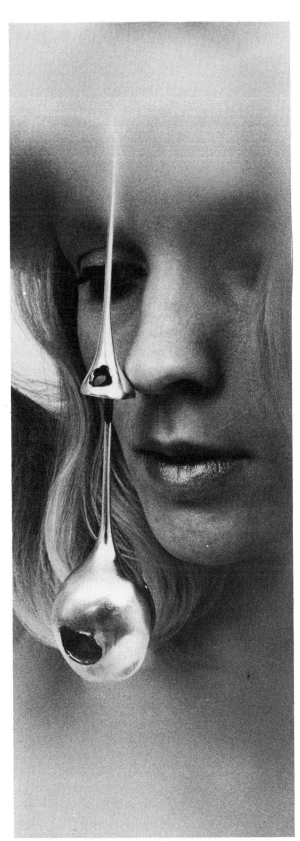

Cast and fabricated sterling silver
pendant with movable base. Cast
from iron prototype.

211

Kauko Moisio

Finland

As another expression in iron, Kauko Moisio builds settings for rock crystal and mercury by using the traditional blacksmith's technique of forging. With this technique, he heats his iron to its malleable point on a coal forge and then hammers, elongates, or "stretches" the iron to a desired form against an anvil. The procedure involves heating, hammering, reheating, rehammering, and so forth, until the form assumes its intended shape. The final form, its surfaces, and its edges are refined by files and by grinding and polishing bits used in an electric drill.

What Kauko does is to forge out a small iron container form. The container is built as a setting for a completely transparent rock crystal of predetermined size. Lately, he's been building his container forms with chambers at more than one level and with an exposed top surface that is left rough or that has even been built with small iron flower-head forms projecting up vertically. Once the iron container has reached its final form, Kauko then partially fills it with a few drops of pure, refined mercury. The container form with the mercury inside is then permanently capped with the rock crystal. Kauko uses a two-component epoxy cement to hold the rock crystal in place. He allows this to harden for several days before moving the completed form.

The result is a cubiclelike form with a transparent windowlike cap. When the form is tipped or moved, the rough or textured top surface of the iron container causes the mercury to split up into separate pools. The chambers within the iron container provide hollows or caves into which the mercury can disappear as the form is moved. To jiggle the form and look down at it through the rock crystal window is to see the mercury continually splitting up, reforming, and even temporarily disappearing into one of the chambers.

When Kauko first began exploring the idea, he ran into problems. Sometimes the crystal would fog up on its undersurface, and at other times, even after the mercury was sealed in, it would change from its bright silver color into a smoke gray. After a number of experiments, Kauko decided that the problems must have arisen either from impurities (dust, iron slag, or foreign particles) mixing with the mercury or from the mercury coming into contact with the epoxy before the rock crystal setting had hardened. To solve the problems, he began to change his iron container so that he formed an extra top lip or frame, which lifted the rock crystal slightly higher and away from the mercury. Then, too, he took extra precautions to insure that the container, the undersurface of the rock crystal, and the epoxy were free of impurities before the mercury was added. Whatever the difficulties may have been, his precautions solved the problem — no more crystal fogging, and no more graying of mercury.

Kauko is well aware of the potential vapor danger when using mercury, and for this reason he stores the mercury in a tightly sealed Pyrex vial at slightly below room temperature, opening the vial only after all stages of form construction have been prepared in advance to receive the pouring in and capping off of the mercury.

His forms thus far have involved only rock crystal caps, but he has lately been giving thought to using blown glass, transparent acryl, prismatic glass, and even a type of magnifying glass cap to enlarge the action of the moving mercury. He says that he's also given thought to building the iron container with a concealed tap or bottom plug so that the mercury can be removed and refreshed or even so that other types of liquids can be inserted into the container.

With his own work, Kauko is much less concerned with the "pure" aesthetics of form than with how he personally caresses or marks his iron with his personality. Above all else, Kauko considers himself a black-smith — "a member of an honorable profession that has unfortunately lost its fashion appeal in the public eye, and particularly in the awarding of public funds for architecture and architectural sculpture." He feels that too few people are aware of the beauty in wrought iron. He, of course, loves his work and his material and feels that iron is in no way inferior to rare, exotic, expensive, or fashionable materials.

Forged iron pendant with rock crystal cap and liquid mercury fill.

Forged iron ring. Rock crystal cap, liquid mercury fill.

Forged iron pendant, second view.

Flemming Hertz
Denmark

Flemming Hertz is both an architect and a designer. One of his recent projects was an attempt to convince the Danish candy industry to produce edible jewelry. The attempt failed.

Is edible jewelry only the gimmick it is claimed to be? A gimmick to be scorned and sneered at? Or is it a feasible possibility?

Flemming Hertz did not invest in his project as a joke. On the contrary, he was entirely serious. He actually constructed sophisticated prototypes and worked from the ground up, coordinating his own efforts with one of the few remaining Danish firms still producing entirely hand-formed candies. His intentions were to produce bold, hard-sugar sculptural forms with explosive colors and to then mount these forms on inexpensive plastic throwaway ring bands.

Flemming's original prototypes were actually much more refined than they appear in the book photographs. Unfortunately, by the time I got around to photographing the models, many of them were well over twelve months old and had been passed from hand to hand or had been left standing on executive desks and window ledges where Flemming had attempted to promote his idea. Understandably, many of the prototypes were a bit wilted. But not all was lost. After the photographing was completed, Flemming and I sat down and ate them. They were delicious!

I am not a full-blooded designer, nor am I a craftsman. The few things I've made — such as the candy jewelry — were simply visions, and I was not really sure if they could be realized. In the case of the candy jewelry, I tried to have them manufactured, but nobody was seriously interested. On other "visionary" projects it has been my experience that there is a long, long road to travel between an idea and the point where the idea is industrially produced. The facts are that traditional production seems almost antivisionary. This has led me to more or less give up designing, except when I meet a specific demand for a project in my professional work as an architect, a project which the existing market does not fulfill. Even in these cases, you mostly find that the answer you get from industrial leaders, or even development people, is that "fame" counts. If they do not know your work, and if your reputation will not provide a built-in sale, they will not even listen to your ideas. I believe this situation is well known to all amateur designers, whereas many professional designers are fighting most of their lives in order to keep from prostituting themselves at the hands of industry. So what do you do? Start a production collective? Start your own factory? Buy shares in the existing system? Give up believing in your own ideas and let the capitalists have their own way? I have no answers to the questions — only the questions. My own private theory is that design is in many ways asocial and not worth using too much time on before we have changed our political circumstances to the point where design can be a natural and uncomplicated part of society.

Edible ring in striped sugar with
plastic throwaway band.

Caramel ring from sugar with
throwaway plastic band.

Caramel ring — sugar with throwaway plastic band.

215

Jeremy Hough
England

Jeremy Hough works with both cybernetics and kinetics. He envisions a real possibility of incorporating these two disciplines within jewelry. With less than peanuts for a budget, Jeremy built several working prototype jewelry forms combining his ideas within these disciplines. His prototypes actually worked. They moved on command, and they flashed colors according to scheme.

Jeremy does not present his explorations as "works of art." On the contrary, he is fully aware of their limitations, and, in some cases, even their imperfections. But Jeremy is trying. In contributing words to this book Jeremy pokes fun at himself, building a self-portrait that combines both the mad scientist and the absent-minded inventor. Are Jeremy's explorations an indication of one future direction for jewelry?

In the early days, when I dared to dream a lot and produce nothing — nothing I felt pleased with — I found myself making up all sorts of arguments for and against art and kinetics which could be played off against one another, visually and verbally inside my mind.

I was my own art show, playing both sides at once. Here I was in my mind, the world-famous artist-inventor putting forward earth-shattering hypotheses to the nation. There I was, talking in hallowed, incomprehensible terms about the life work of this great man. I would be the subject, the critic, the fanatic masses, the music, and the film all at once. But it never got me anywhere, because I was the only one who knew about it.

Later, while on the journey through art school, I began to put together a master plan for the kind of work that was likely to fulfill some of my ideals.

The way the artist ought to move (the artist being the one who makes his or her craft into a fine art) according to my master plan, was toward an understanding of the environment and all its components. Some of those components, useful and insignificant in their ordinary workaday role, when taken out of context, become very special, quite possibly works of art. Well, we all know that, you might say — most sculptures since the Duchamp "readymades" have echoed this. But my plan was to use a great number of environmental components — light, movement, color, form, space, sound mobility, life — in a way which would come close to returning them to originality while at the same time remaining aloof from reality.

Unfortunately the cost of all this is beyond the ordinary art student's bank account, but I found it possible to begin to put the plan itself into operation on a smaller scale. Although in the dream everything was massive, perfect, and amazing, when reality dawned, the actual work I produced and became involved with was jewelry — very small, and grossly imperfect; nevertheless, although not amazing, it was praised from far and near as "interesting."

Suspecting, in my naiveté, that such praise could be the threshold of success, the ideas took me to electronics companies, influential people, and galleries — all of whom found it strangely matter-of-fact to shatter illusions out of hand. Electronics companies suffer from astronomical tooling costs; influential people suffer from sudden spurts of noninfluentiality; and private galleries, apparently, have to be given leave to sell any exhibited work — even the national art associations have waiting lists that are years long.

What then was the dejected dreamer to do? Raid the most famous London galleries of modern art on press day — that's what!

Too late to catch the Hayward Gallery's world kinetic show, so my attention was turned to the ICA's "Electric Theatre" exhibition.

The new plan was to pass in with the general crowd "armed to the teeth" with specially designed "photo-flood hand-grenades," noise-generating pods, and motorized units — all of which could be taken from their attaché case and released into the darkness and the unsuspecting attention of the press people busying themselves with their notebooks and cameras. A master plan on all counts.

Enthusiastically, I made a prototype "light grenade" cheap enough to be cast into the darkness for its one moment of glory before being squashed by unseen size nines or confiscated by officialdom. But alas, the exhibition opened during my vacation, and I was living on an overdraft anyway.

Much later, and feeling a little lost on a course he couldn't understand, our young dreamer turned his attention to theory, thereby shelving all those "interesting" ideas in order to begin a new plan: the Ultimate Mobile Kinetic Show.

Briefly, it incorporates such traits as an entire body outfit — a kind of BBC "Cyberman" if you like — where jewelry or body adornment, as such, becomes everything. It takes over the entire person, but whatever it does, however massive, perfect, or amazing, the wearer will control it, and the wearer will become the work of art. Free to roam anywhere. Free from the fight for recognition.

Red and green perspex brooch. This is a machined block of perspex that contains a mercury battery, a manual rotary switch, a complicated electronic circuit, and 6 red solid-state lamps. The lamps are each held in 18-carat gold tubes. The lamps twinkle in a semirandom pattern.

Red and silver hexagon bangle.
Silver was folded and fitted around
sawed blocks of perspex. The unit
contains 2 large transistor circuits,
4 rechargeable cells, 12 miniature
incandescent lamps, 2 magnetic
switches, a sealed sliding compart-
ment, and 2 meters of insulated
copper wire. The lamps flash in
alternate corners on both sides at
one second intervals.

Red and silver hexagon bangle,
detail.

Orange perspex and stainless steel
articulating neckpiece. The large
pendant pivots on the "stetho-
scope" neckpiece. As the pendant
pivots electrically, the 4 built-in
incandescent lamps also blink to
illuminate the sides of the perspex
and the garment of the wearer.

Orange perspex and stainless steel
neckpiece. The perspex block
contains a large transistor circuit, 2
rechargeable cells, a manual rotary
switch, and 2 miniature incandescent lamps. The battery can be
recharged via a socket built into the
bottom end of each tube. When
first switched on, the lamps form
two alternating pools of light that
appear to roll back and forth across
the bottom of the perspex; but as
the switch is turned further, the
lamps flash faster until they both
appear to be on at once. The unit is
worn by springing apart the tubes.

Gijs Bakker
and Emmy Van Leersum
Holland

Are the forms of Gijs Bakker and Emmy Van Leersum only a curiosity? Or are they one valid alternative to the monotonous visual and emotional prison that most of us are locked within? If they are not just a curiosity, then why is it that we so often look at these forms in the same way that we might look at a duck-billed platypus waddling down the main street of Salinas, Kansas? Or as we might look at an accident, a bullfight, or a war? Yes, we *look,* but how often do we really *see, touch,* and then try reality on for size?

These are but a few of the questions that Gijs and Emmy must face every time they produce something new. They are the same questions that all of us must face whenever we take a risk. Gijs and Emmy have obviously taken many risks — public risks, publicity risks, and risks within their own profession. They've leaned their necks way out over dozens of guillotines, and obviously, there are willing executioners waiting to spring out from behind every bush. But how many of the executioners are prepared to deal with the reality of the forms, rather than the verbalism or the intellectualism that the forms provoke?

Gijs and Emmy are involved in creating a dialogue between the garment and the body and between the body and its environment. The cleanliness, or geometry, of their forms is self-evident. Must one always hide the body, cover it up, or translate it into something other than what it is? Or, can cleanliness, as expressed by Gijs and Emmy, be a way of admitting the existence of the body without the need for apology?

That their forms provoke response is undisputable. One could challenge, question, and attack these forms from dozens of angles. But to do so would be to deny Gijs and Emmy their right to design alternatives, while at the same time placing us in the position of manning the guillotine and becoming the unmerciful critics that we are ourselves basically opposed to. Gijs contributes these words for our digestion.

We both feel a heaviness about trying to verbalize our work. Emmy and I have worked together since 1966, and right from the beginning there were many reasons to make what we have made. Emmy and I are very different in character and temperament, but in the end we see and expect something which is equal for both of us. We like to say things in a very clear way without frills around it. We feel that the object (form) must be so simple that it presents a shock, so that people begin to really think. I realize how dangerous it is to use the word "simple," but I do so in the sense that we try to concentrate many thoughts and feelings visually into one logical form on a geometrical base. This is our challenge. A kind of game for us. The form should not be "created." It should come forth naturally as a result of research. The form is, after all, only the wrapping for an idea.

220

We studied at the Art School in Amsterdam in the silversmith department and learned how to make complicated jewelry with expensive stones. While we were doing this, we both asked ourselves, "Why do we make this stuff when we ourselves don't even like to wear it?" We found out. We found out that much of this jewelry was being made for very rich and very old women. We found out that there were more interesting things in life for a young artist than to work for an uninteresting audience. If we had worked for this audience, we would have felt that our work was superfluous.

Jewelry designers are mostly moles, digging under the ground and rarely if ever seeing what's happening all around them. We wanted to get the jewel out of this sphere — to give it a new function more fitting in our time. When someone wears a piece of jewelry, it becomes part of his body. Together with clothes, it gives him the possibility to show to other people who he or she is. We think that it is very important to work on this, to give people some clear alternative which helps them to discover themselves and helps them to show who they are.

With this in mind, we made large aluminum shoulder pieces in 1967 as a contrast (demonstration) to the "gala-collier," or diadem, we all know. Our collars should, notwithstanding their format, have an interesting relationship to the body, bringing out, rather than dominating, its beauty. Emmy always used to say that everybody is beautiful, and that it's only our frustrations that make us ugly. I'm sure she's right. We remarked that when people wear our aluminum collars they have to walk straight on with their heads — to take away their hair, expose their faces, and so forth. Most of us have been frustrated by ridiculous fashion magazines that try to convince us to look like someone else. Most of us work very hard to look like someone else, but we forget ourselves. And then all of those things which don't fit into the person we'd like to be end up as characteristics we feel we must hide. This is what makes us ugly.

When we first exhibited our clothing, we used professional models based on the same visual idea as our jewelry. But when we exhibited our clothing in 1970, we stopped using models. What we did was to ask all of our friends to wear our clothes. When the exhibition opened, it turned into an unplanned "happening." Our friends and the visiting public all came in at the same time. It was a shocking confrontation. Why is it more difficult to wear something on the body than to hang another something — a painting, for example — on the wall?

Aluminum shoulder piece.

Aluminum collar.

Aluminum collar and dress.

222

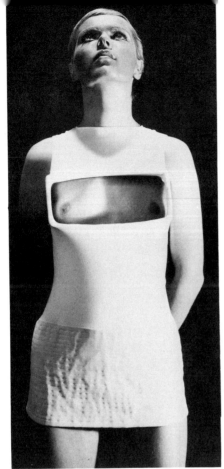

Prototype body form.

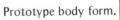

Prototype body form.

Prototype body form.

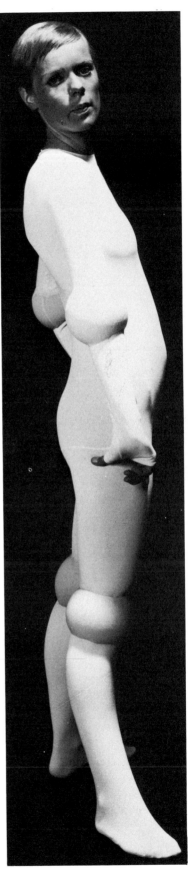

223

Prototype body forms. Knitted in
circle with elastic synthetic fiber.
Rings are permanently sewn in
place to accent the forms and
provide freedom of movement.

Prototype body form, detail.

Prototype body form, detail.

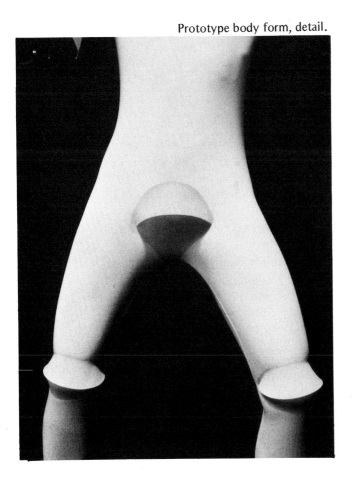

Prototype body form, detail.

225

Additional Contributors

The gathering together of craftsmen from all parts of the world is no simple task. There are obvious problems. One of them is the problem of great distances and the need for communication via correspondence. Inevitably, there are communication breaks between craftsman and author. Such breaks have many causes: lost letters, unanswered correspondence, photography mixups, economic stress, and even work or teaching demands that have become overly taxing on the individual.

Our own effort was not without a few of these unavoidable communication breaks. For example, Americans Jakobine Hobbs and Joan Ann Jablow both contributed examples of their forms but no essay material. The same was true for our three contributors from Japan: Yasuki Hiramatsu, Eugene Pijanowski, and Hiroko Sato Pijanowski. Somewhere along the line of communication between Japan, Denmark, and the United States there was a mixup. Yasuki Hiramatsu is an assistant professor at Tokyo Geijutsu University. As for Eugene and Hiroko Sato Pijanowski, Eugene is an American and his wife is Japanese. Both of them studied at Cranbrook Academy of Art in America, but now live and work in Japan.

Even without mentioning it, it ought to be self-evident that those of us involved in this book do not by any stretch of the imagination represent ourselves to be the last word in jewelry form-making. We are but a representative sampling of what's going on around the world. Hopefully, there are hundreds of other craftsmen performing on levels equal — or perhaps even superior — to what we herein represent. Obviously, it would be impossible to find all of the inventive jewelry craftsmen in the world, and even more impossible to include them all under one book cover. To those craftsmen who have been omitted, overlooked, or otherwise undiscovered — we all join in extending encouragement.

Photography Credits

In addition to the many craftsmen who photographed their own work, grateful acknowledgment is extended to the following photographers and institutions:

Anne Havgaard, Denmark
Solvhjem, Denmark
Winifred Zakovski, Finland
Borje Ronnberg, Norway
Jaap de Graaf, Holland
Matthijs Schrofer, Holland
Sebastian Schroder, Switzerland
Tilmann Gasch, Germany
National Palace Museum, Republic of China

British Steel Corporation, England
Electrum Gallery, England
Pip Benveniste, England
Adrian Swinstead, England
Horst Kolo, England
Mike Beringer, England

Ogilvy and Mather, Ltd., England
The Worshipful Company of Goldsmiths, England
The American Craftsman's Council, United States
John Daughtry, United States
True Kelly, United States
Chuck Simmons, United States
Hosea Fumero, United States
Jerrold Cohen, United States
Camera Crafts Studio, United States
Bob Hanson, United States
Ferdinand Boesch, United States
Lida Moser, United States
Betsey Bess, United States
William G. Larson, United States
Vanguard Photography, United States